ALL Y

SHELJA SEN lives in Delhi with her husband, Amit, and two vibrant children, Nishat and Anya. She is a child & adolescent psychologist and family therapist. She loves children and believes that more than professional training (an MPhil and Doctorate in Clinical Psychology), the children – hers as well and those of other parents – she has worked with for over two decades, are the ones who taught her about life.

Shelja has co-founded Children First, an institute for child & adolescent mental health and she also practises there. She holds workshops and writes regular columns on parenting. Her passion pushed her to write this book in which she shares the five anchors of parenting. She believes that parenting is not about fixing the child but growing up and empowering ourselves for this journey. Shelja also loves the outdoors and enjoys listening to music, watching movies, baking, dancing, reading books and writing. You could write to her at shelja.sen@childrenfirstindia.com or visit Children First at www.childrenfirstindia.com

ALL YOU NEED IS LOVE

The Art of Mindful Parenting

SHELJA SEN

Collins

First published in India in 2015 by Collins
An imprint of HarperCollins *Publishers*

Copyright © Shelja Sen 2015

P-ISBN: 978-93-5177-072-5
E-ISBN: 978-93-5177-073-2

2 4 6 8 10 9 7 5 3 1

Shelja Sen asserts the moral right
to be identified as the author of this work.

HarperCollins *Publishers*
A-75, Sector 57, Noida, Uttar Pradesh 201301, India
1 London Bridge Street, London, SE1 9GF, United Kingdom
Hazelton Lanes, 55 Avenue Road, Suite 2900, Toronto, Ontario M5R 3L2
and 1995 Markham Road, Scarborough, Ontario M1B 5M8, Canada
25 Ryde Road, Pymble, Sydney, NSW 2073, Australia
195 Broadway, New York, NY 10007, USA

Typeset in 11.5/15 Elegant Garamond BT by
R. Ajith Kumar

Printed and bound at
Thomson Press (India) Ltd

To
*Nishat and Anya, who helped me dig deep and scale
new heights. I love you all the way to the end of the
universe and back.*

*To Amit, who taught me the meaning of,
'All you need is love'.*

I accept and love you the way you are. You are unique, you are different and you are you. I will not compare you with others, I will not constantly keep expecting and demanding what you might not be able to do or give.

CONTENTS

INTRODUCTION

I was very confident about parenting before I had children of my own. When people approached me with their concerns, I knew exactly what to say to them. However, things changed dramatically after I became a parent. I do not think anything in this world comes close to changing us as a person or our lives as much as having children. Bill O. Hanlon, the famous psychotherapist, told us an interesting story in one of his workshops. He talked about a man who ran a parenting workshop called Ten Commandments of Parenting. After his marriage, he decided to call it Five Suggestions on Parenting. Soon he had a baby and he changed the workshop's name to Three Tips on Parenting. Then he had twins and he gave it up altogether!

Therefore, at the outset, let me clarify that I do not want to pose as a parenting expert. Far from it! This book is about sharing my own journey with you in a voice that is my own. There is nothing in the world I feel more passionately about than children and parenting. I have read, reflected, and pondered over this for many years. Parenting has by far been my most courageous and meaningful endeavour. I have learned a lot from children and families I have worked with over the years. I have made mistakes – colossal ones – in bringing up my children, especially my elder one, who has, in his own inimitable way, forgiven me ('I was your guinea pig, Mum, you didn't know any better then!'). Parenting has brought out the most intense emotions in me – excruciating pain, frazzled nerves, paralysing anxiety and soul-wrecking guilt. However, all those have been outweighed by immense joy, gratitude and love.

It's Not About Them, It's About Us

I believe that parenting is not about the techniques but our philosophy of life in general. It's not about our children but about our becoming more aware, mindful, sensitive and conscious human beings. It's also about the life lessons we learn on the way that go on to become the most precious gift from our children.

The Inside-out Approach

I do not think that parenting comes naturally to all of us. There are some earth mothers and fathers, who seem to be made for parenting. They are nurturers and their patience, calmness and gentle presence (amidst all the chaos) is amazing. For the rest of us, we have to develop these skills and way of being through a lot of conscious reflection and soul-searching. Parenting has been one of the most healing processes for me. Through it I have understood my deepest fears, my vulnerabilities, my passions and my strengths. Therefore I do believe, very strongly, that parenting has to be an inside-out process. As parents, we have to go with the principle that I have to first work on myself. Whatever issues you might be facing with your child, the question is not what your child needs to do, but what you need to reflect on or do as a parent. If you are facing a difficulty with your child, ask yourself these questions, 'How do I feel about it?' 'How is that impacting my child?' 'Is it my need or my child's?' 'What do I need to do as a parent?' Answer these questions with honesty and courage and you will know what to do. It sounds a little tricky but let me try to explain with the help of an example. Let us assume your child is very shy. Rather than pushing her to speak up in a social situation, you reflect on why you might be uncomfortable with her shyness and whether it is your need or hers to be socially confident. Therefore, parenting is not about them, it's about us. It is our opportunity for mental, emotional and spiritual awakening.

Each Child is Wired and Inspired Differently

I accept and love you the way you are. You are unique, you are different and you are you. I will not compare you with others, I will not constantly keep expecting and demanding what you might not be able to do or give.

We have seven children in our extended family, including my children, nephews and nieces. Titli, at nineteen, is graceful, poised, a deep sea diver and a beautiful dancer; Tan, eighteen, is a charming, vibrant young man with a keen ear for music; Tia (Tan's twin) is wild, vivacious and the artist of the family; Joey, at seventeen, is adventurous, an independent thinker and a zealous wildlife enthusiast. Sixteen-year-old Nishat is a deep thinker and writer, a marine-life enthusiast and a passionate actor, while Sushrut, sixteen, is sporty, loves music, is focused and thriving academically. Twelve-year-old Anya, who is mature beyond her years, is an avid animal lover who livens up our home with her heart-warming guitar strumming and lilting voice. Each one is so different from the other and so amazing in his or her own way. I cannot expect Tan to belt out poetry like Nishat just as I cannot expect Nishat to be the life of a party like Tan. At the core of parenting (or any relationship for that matter), there needs to be acceptance. That and a love for what is, rather than constantly struggling and fighting for what isn't. No matter how hard I try, I cannot make a cat bark or an oak sapling grow to be a banyan tree. If we just stopped resisting and fighting reality then parenting won't remain such a battle any more.

What We Focus on Grows

This is so simple and yet so true. Buddhist Zen master Thich Nhat Hanh describes beautifully how each one of us have both negative seeds (anger, rage, jealousy, hatred) and wholesome seeds (love, joy, gratitude, compassion, courage).

According to him, what will blossom depends on the seeds we water and nurture. Similarly, in our relationship with our children, we end up either watering their negative seeds or wholesome ones. And what we will focus on will grow. This goes very much against the common parenting practice of 'fix the child'. In our anxiety to 'correct' them, we end up lecturing them on their irresponsible lifestyle, fixing tuition teachers for all the subjects they are weak in or criticizing them on their wrong choices. The more problems we see, the more we crank up our negativity. I believe that if we learned to accept the child as he is and directed our attention to what he can do, it will help him grow much more than if we focused only on what he cannot do. I read somewhere, 'There is nothing wrong with you that the right with you cannot fix.' This will become clearer as you read the rest of the book.

Children Will Do Well If They Can

Every child is wired to grow, explore, learn and flourish. Look at the baby who is learning to walk, he takes a tentative step forward, looks at his parents with a proud smile, takes another step and then, maybe, falls down. He laughs, clambers up again to take a few steps and then falls again. This goes on for some time till he is tired, sleepy and, after a good rest, starts all over again. There is no sense of embarrassment, shame or self-doubt. So where does it start going wrong? Let us take the example of the same baby again. What if we started to tell the baby that he has to try harder, make sure he bends forward, or that if he straightens his knees a little or looks forward he might move better. Or if we started comparing his steps to our friend's daughter who, at the same age, is running. I am sure very soon he might give up and not want to try much. We might dismiss his lack of effort as 'does not want to try', 'wants to take the easy way out', 'is plain lazy' or 'wants to waste his life just doing nothing'.

Sounds quite ridiculous, right? But that's exactly what we are doing with our older children. Whenever they stop trying or moving forward we want to immediately label them without finding out why it is happening. 'He wants to waste his life,' 'She just does not want to try,' 'He is just not bothered!'

Is it the wiring that is stopping the child from learning? For example, just by criticizing, we cannot expect a child with dyslexia to start reading or one with attention deficit disorder (ADD) to start paying attention in class.

Is it self-doubt, a low sense of worthiness that is stopping the child from keeping pace with his peer group? Maybe, emotionally, the child is not in a good space due to problems at home or difficulties with friends in school. There could be a myriad reasons why the child is not doing well but it can never be that he does not want to or that he just wants to waste his life away.

I have always been a little flummoxed by a lot of parenting literature out there which aims at categorizing parents into pigeonholes on the basis of parenting styles. So we hear a lot about different styles of parenting: permissive, laissez-faire, helicopter, drill sergeant, tiger mom, authoritarian, authoritative, democratic, etc. I have never known which style I fit into till the realization hit me that I do not have to be boxed into any. There is no cookie-cutter approach to parenting. I am fine as I am and my own style of parenting, with all its imperfections, works well too. It has been so liberating to give myself permission to be imperfect. Parents already feel judged and we do not have to add to that burden by slotting them into boxes. There is no right or wrong way of parenting. If each child is wired and inspired differently, then each parent is wired and inspired differently too.

So, this book is not about making you a perfect parent so

that you can have perfect kids. In this world of overloaded information and overscheduled, overprotected children, I do not promise you any fun, fast and easy ways or quick fixes. This is not another preachy book that will make you feel guiltier as a parent or more anxious about how you are not getting it right. I hope it will be like a companion for you to reflect, introspect and dig deep to connect to the immense wealth of wisdom that is already there.

I have tried to reduce the clutter in my narrative by not bringing in reams of research in every chapter. Instead, I have included them in my reading list at the end of the book. I personally do not like to use he/she so have used he or she according to what came naturally to me at that time and not in any way to indicate any gender specificity. I have added Reflections, little pauses where you can sit back, think through, mull over and internalize some of the concepts that I would be highlighting. I have been able to gain maximum from books where I have highlighted, written little notes in the margins, reflected in a separate journal, deliberated over the ideas and woven them into some of my own. I would strongly recommend that to all the readers. Read, make notes, highlight, and discuss with your spouses, your children and your friends. Reflect, metabolize and make the learnings your own.

I have divided the rest of the book into, what I think, are the five anchors of parenting – Connect, Coach, Care, Community and Commit. They are all interlinked and flow from one to another. Connect is the keystone, the foundation, the essential ingredient of parenting. It is about laying down nourishing soil replete with love, worthiness, joy, recognitions and positive energy. Coaching is about building necessary life skills in children through an understanding of their unique wiring and temperament. Care is about nurturing ourselves for a more wholesome life. Community is about building caring ecosystems for children to thrive in. Commit is about sustaining the courage and compassion for our whole-hearted journey.

Parenting is not just about bringing up children. It is about growing up and transforming ourselves to be better human beings. It is not about teaching but about learning from our children. In that sense I am making a paradigm shift, as I believe that parenting is a voyage we take to explore our own internal terrain of emotional wounds. It is about soothing these wounds and discovering deep wisdom within. It is about embarking on a soul journey, which despite its heartache and gut-wrenching pain, will heal and fulfil us at every step.

1

CONNECT

Connect is the essence of any relationship. It is the core, the heart of what makes a relationship work. It is the deep, pulsating, positive energy that flows between people. It is about the bond that we create between our heart and the child's. It is our ability to connect to the child's essence at a cellular level. Connect is not about teaching or doing, it is about *just being* and celebrating the child as she is. It is not about the child you wished you had or the one you hope you can have but the one in front of you. 'I love you as you are and not as I wish you were!'

I really like the way social researcher Brené Brown describes it as making the child feel 'worthy as you are' in her book, *The Gifts of Imperfection*. It is not when you score higher, become prettier, dance better or become more popular; it is just 'as you are' right now.

I know it is not as easy as it sounds. You do not have a baby and declare, 'I am going to love you just the way you are' and pronto, you find your Connect and live happily ever after. I like to believe that Connect is a direction and not a destination. Connect is not a switch you flip on and let the juices of love flow. There are times when it flows, at times it spurts and at times it is just a little trickle that you squeeze out of your weary soul. It requires grit and gumption to hold on to it at every step.

As a parent I have learned one thing – whenever I hit a roadblock with either of my children, I always ask myself – 'How is my Connect right now?' More often than not, I notice that a Disconnect has, in some way, seeped in. Maybe I have been pre-occupied with a project, not spending time with them, being a little snappy, demanding more than giving.

One clichéd analogy (but so true!) I like to use is how we can see our relationship with our children like an emotional bank account – where we make deposits (hugging, kissing, cuddling, recognizing, having fun times) and from which we make withdrawals (questioning, ordering, comparing, demanding, criticizing, shouting, behaving in a hostile manner). As long as the deposits outweigh the withdrawals, our Connect is generally going strong. However, as soon as the withdrawals start accruing and the deposits start dwindling, the Disconnect starts to make its presence felt in the form of rudeness and the child answering back with, 'I don't have to listen to you,' 'You don't understand' and 'I'm outta here.'

Higher the withdrawal, higher the Disconnect and more severe the difficulties – rudeness, rebellion, anger, lying, stealing. So if your child is showing any of these characteristics, don't worry about the behaviour – look beneath the façade and you will see a person who is emotionally vulnerable and hanging on to the threads of Disconnect.

Going back to the 'Inside-out' approach that I highlighted in the Introduction, it is important for us to reflect on what causes this Disconnect.

What Causes Disconnect?

Our inadequacies

We are all wounded or hurt in some way or the other. We carry the pain from these wounds, sometimes transgenerational, for most of our lives. We cover them with socially appropriate masks, which serve us fine most of the time. But somehow, parenting peels away the mask and leaves us raw and vulnerable. A crying baby who will not settle down, a toddler who refuses to eat, a little one who is not able to make friends or a teenager who is just not performing can leave us feeling very inadequate and not good enough. This feeling of ineptitude can start a vicious downward spiral of self-doubt, fears that turn to anger, maybe rage, at the child for not delivering, finally leading to guilt and then to inadequacy. It is not possible to build a Connect when we come from a position of inadequacy and scarcity. Parenting is a great opportunity for us to face our inadequacies directly and heal.

Non-acceptance of 'What Is'

We might deny it to the world all we like but we know that right from the time our babies are born, we know what we want them to grow up to be. Sometimes these visions are clear and precise: doctor; engineer; MBA; lawyer; architect, and sometimes these are loose wishful, wistful thoughts: take dance lessons as I never could; be fair and tall; top the class in math; play football like me. It could be as simple (or complex) as having a child of a particular gender. There are expectations, hopes, prospects, dreams that we are programmed to start nurturing from the time we think of having a baby.

I call these dreams irrational, as they actually make no sense. How can I, as a parent, decide what my child will grow up to be? How can I, as a parent, foist my dreams on my child? We don't want to accept it but that's what we are doing all the time. How much does our measure of who we are come from our children's achievements? How difficult is it for us to step back and let our children be who they are? We bestow upon them our own unresolved needs, frustrated dreams and unrealized expectations. We do not stay with 'what is' and keep going over and over again about 'what could have been'.

What happens to us when we have a child who is very different from our dream child? What happens when she does not look like we had hoped she would, get scores the way we aspired to, or have dreams of doing things that are not in keeping with ours? Some of us are able to accept it, some even learn to celebrate it but a lot of us stay with our unmetabolized hopes and let it sour our relationship and cause a Disconnect.

Fixed social narratives

Our society has very strong beliefs or what I call fixed narratives about what makes 'good children'. Such children have to be fair and lovely, good looking, charming, outgoing, intelligent, talented, well behaved, compliant, confident, score good marks and so on and so forth. These are the round holes we have prepared for them en masse, and all the kids have to do is slide down and fit themselves into the holes. Some do so marvellously and some have to be pushed, pulled, poked and pressed till they fit in. However, there are some who just do not – the proverbial square pegs. According to the society, they are neither fair, nor good looking, pretty, intelligent, talented, well behaved and confident. The series of nots keep multiplying as they grow older. They are not valued or appreciated by the society. We as parents tend to see our children through the same faulty lens provided by the society. No wonder we feel disappointed in them from a very early age when they do not measure up to the benchmark set by society.

Parental stress

Higher the level of stress the parent is going through, more vulnerable the child becomes to Disconnect. As a parent I know that every time I have sensed a Disconnect with either of my children, it has always been due to some kind of stress I was going through in life. So, now, whenever I see either of my children being rude/indifferent/irritable with me, I immediately check my own stress level. Am I reflecting some of my strain on them? Am I preoccupied with something else when I am with them? This is what I call the 'parental mindful meter'. That's the inside-out approach where, before you blame the child, you pause and look inside yourself.

Daily demands

Most of the time, it is the mundane daily *khit pit* (petty arguments) that drains the emotional bank account. We get so lost in our role and day-to-day agenda that we end up failing to get the big picture. Imagine what a typical child might have to go through every day.

'Get up otherwise you will miss the bus.'

'Have you brushed your teeth properly?'

'Why didn't you pack your bag last night?'

'Stop playing around with your breakfast.'

'Don't lose your water bottle again!'

'Remember to eat your lunch.'

'Write down all your homework in the diary.'

'If you miss your bus today, I am not going to drop you to school.'

Phew! Imagine having to go through something like this every day of your life! No wonder, after some time, children develop this 'I am not bothered' attitude in an attempt to avoid the daily bickering.

I read about this research where a group of children were taken to a neuroscience lab. Their brains were connected to machines to check the electrical activity for various stimuli. They found that there was no brain activity when they were presented with their mother's nagging voice. Not even a little spark! Children learn to filter out their parent's voice (I am sure Dads would have the same experience if they took on a more active role in nagging, sorry, parenting!) from a very early age. Then we complain that they are not listening!

Life experiences

At times, love cannot flow naturally and it could be because of difficult life experiences. Maybe this is a pregnancy you never wanted, or a birth that left you with post-partum depression. There might have been loss, bereavement, financial strain, or an acrimonious divorce. These experiences can sap you of energy, leaving you wrenched and bereft of the basic vitality that Connect requires. I know all of us have heard of experiences where some of the severest losses and disasters have not impacted the Connect at all and maybe made it even stronger. There are inspirational stories that come from extraordinary people at extraordinary times.

Shame language

'Are you shaming your kids?'

When I ask most parents this question, their immediate response is, 'No'. However, what if I asked you to go through the questions/statements and tell me if you use them with your kids?

'Why can't you understand something so simple?'

'Why can't you be like your sister?'

'Why are you so slow?'

'Don't be so messy!'

Along with, maybe, rolling eyes, a clenched jaw and an exasperated look. I am talking about mild statements which are the repertoire of most parents' daily interaction with their children. If you look at these statements or body language, you will find mild traces of shame in each one of them. I am not even getting into hard-core shaming like using words like 'stupid', 'idiot', 'good-for-nothing' with hitting, pushing, cold silences or abuses that might go on in many homes.

We live in a society where peppering our vocabulary with abusive words is the done thing – a father might reprimand his son, calling him a 'dimwit'. And I am still within the realm of what is concerned as reasonably polite, in public, with nobody batting an eyelid! Go behind the doors and the exchanges can become more sick, lethal and toxic. What is the harm, you might ask? It is believed that parents want and know what is best for their children so what is wrong with a little shaming every now and then?

According to Brené, shaming is one of the top parenting and teaching strategies. I couldn't agree more. It comes so naturally to us that it is automatically ingrained in our parenting style. We were raised like this, we see it around us and we take the shaming tradition forward. We all carry shame in some form or the other from childhood. It could range from looks, low scores, which neighbourhood you lived in, fights at home, family secrets, sexual abuse, family finances, etc. We learn not to talk about it and stay silent. However, that does not let the shame go away, it festers, grows and multiplies inside us. So it's not much of a surprise why most of us grow up with a sense of inadequacy and the feeling, 'I am not good enough'. To hide this, we learn to hustle by pleasing, performing, proving and perfecting. Or, on the other hand, we deal with it by moving away, reacting and rebelling. Sometimes these patterns continue for a lifetime. Despite what we do to mask it, we manage to live our lives, never being able to feel worthy of who we are.

Go back to your childhood and think about a shameful memory. It could be mocking words uttered by a bully, an insensitive teacher or a raging parent. Today, the words might still ring in your head with the same clarity. Brené distinguishes between humiliation and shame by explaining the former as 'something bad happened to me', but the latter as 'I am bad'. A child who is shouted at by her teacher might feel humiliated and come back and talk to her mother about it, 'I know I had not done my homework but she should not have shouted at me like that in front of everybody.' On the other hand, the child who feels shame does not come home and talk about it at all because she feels she is bad and she deserved it. Therefore shame breeds in secrecy and silence.

Words play an important role in our world and relationships. Derogatory words can lower our *prana* or *chi*. It is impossible to be offensive and spiritually aware or evolved at the same time. Being vicious towards somebody pulls us down to a low level of consciousness where we might feel cut off from feelings of compassion or our own wisdom.

In my house, we have very clear rules as far as language is concerned. Words like 'shut up', 'idiot' and 'stupid' are a complete no-no. And if my kids are having a fight they are allowed to be very creative in expressing their feelings to each other without using any abusive words. So most of the time the slanging match easily turns into a Dr Seuss-style repartee full of ingenuity, wit and humour.

How Can We Build Connect?

Some of you might be wandering about in the land of Disconnect for some time, looking for ways to find your way back home while some of you might be teetering on the edge. There might be many who have a Connect and are looking for ways to make it even stronger. So how can we build one?

Mindfulness

Parenting is an inside job. For that we have to calm our chattering mind and connect with the deep wisdom within. This can only happen through mindfulness, which is about slowing down our minds and freeing our mental space. It is about being present to ourselves and to our children in the here and now. When we are less mindful and more mindless, parenting can become a knee-jerk reaction. However, when we are more mindful, we create the inner space to reach out to our own wisdom and respond with clear thinking, understanding and acceptance of 'what is'. I have observed that my mindlessness hooks my children's mindlessness. However, if I stay mindful, it immediately has a similar effect on them. Therefore, as I mentioned earlier, keep track of your mindfulness through what I call the 'parenting mindful meter'. It is mindfulness that helps a parent become aware and navigate through her own inadequacies, non-acceptance, stress, fixed social narratives, negative life experiences and her own hurtful language to build a genuine connect with her child. I do firmly believe that mindfulness is a necessary pre-requisite to meaningful parenting or, in fact, any meaningful relationship.

Reflection

Just stop here for a moment and reflect on your mindful meter. Where are you right now on a scale of 0 to 10?

If it is a number lower down on the scale you might experience scattered, stressed or antsy feelings. Take a deep breath and become aware of your own feelings. Label these feelings like this:

'I can see I am feeling really annoyed right now.'

'Ah, here comes my old friend worry, wonder what it has to say today.'

As you become aware of these feelings, see them slowly fade away. Take a deep breath and focus your mind on something that gives you a feeling of immense pleasure, love and a sense of gratitude. Amp it up till you start feeling it in every cell of your body. It could actually give you a tingling sensation. Enjoy that sensation and then go back and check your mindful meter again. Do not give up if you feel that it has not gone up very high. Mindfulness is also a skill that takes time to develop. Carry that mindful meter with you and you will start noticing the difference. You could use certain cues to help you initially – every time your mobile rings or the number of times you stop at a traffic light. Whenever I am interacting with my children (I do slip ever so often, I must admit) and sense an irritation or annoyance in myself, I try to put a check on my mindful meter. As soon as I label my feeling, I see it slowly dissolve (most of the times) and I am ready to be present to them more mindfully rather than just react mindlessly.

Time

Time is an extremely important ingredient for building Connect. Many of us might be spending time around our kids but how much time are we actually using to Connect with them? I know I struggle with it all the time. I am a solitary person at heart and I really crave to spend time on my own, just reading, reflecting, ideating, creating and writing. And sometimes, as a parent, it is such a wrench to leave that world and give my kids my 100 per cent.

Being with the kids means to immerse ourselves completely in their world – where there is no time for a quick peep into our iPhones, or shooting off a quick email. We know through research about the myth of 'effective multitasking'. When we do two or more things at the same time, we are actually diluting our attention in each area. So if you think you are spending time with the kids while you catch the 9 o'clock news or send messages to your friends on WhatsApp, you might have to do a rethink about your Connect time.

You might think it odd but I like to schedule my time with my kids – after I return from work and till they go to sleep I count as my Connect time. Now I don't mean that in all those four or five hours I am doing a focused one to one with them, but I am there for them if they need me. I might sit and chat with them about their day, supervise their homework, maybe skip into the kitchen to bake a cake, rustle up a small snack or answer some important messages. I generally do not take or make any calls during this time. I know a lot of people get upset with me about this but I have learned to live with that.

The thing with kids, especially teenagers, is that you can't fix a time to talk to them. I might be worrying about why my latest cake recipe isn't working when my sixteen year old might want to talk to me about something that is troubling him. If I tell him at that time that I am busy and maybe we could talk some other day, I might lose out on a wonderful opportunity to have a meaningful chat. Having said that, it might be impossible to switch off immediately from what you are doing. If you are cooking a meal for the family then you cannot drop everything to give uninterrupted time to him. Maybe then, it might work to tell him, 'I would love to talk to you, so let me just finish cooking. Give me half an hour, let's say, 7 o'clock, and I will be with you.'

Some extremely honest mothers have admitted to me that they find it so boring to play with their little children. I can totally empathize with them because I remember thinking once, while playing with my two-year-old son, 'I will go mad if I have to play this dinosaur game again for the tenth time today!' So please don't die of guilt if you find it difficult to play with your children. Find mini-slots of time when you play with her for half an hour and then move away to do something that gives you some respite. Despite popular belief, children need to spend some time on their own, playing. It helps them build their internal world.

I feel that one fall out of new-age parenting is that we think it is our responsibility to entertain our children. From the day they are born we try to be multimedia entertainers for them. They just have to utter the dreaded B word, 'Mum, I'm bored', especially in their whiney, demanding voice, and we seem to hit the panic button. It is as if by saying they are bored, they are just showing us how inadequate we have been as parents. Up we jump, belting out options, 'You want to draw/dance/paint/sing and so on and so forth?' Well, I have a suggestion, next time they say the B word, take a deep breath, relax, smile and say, 'What would you like to do about it?' I know it will be a bit tough initially, after all they are not used to taking charge of their own time. But hang in there, give them time and soon you will find their creative juices overflowing.

From the time my children were little, I have been very clear about 'me time'. My kids know that when I am snuggled in some corner of the house with a book, it is best to leave me alone. Otherwise I can start growling really loudly. That's something they have had to learn about me from the time they were babies. And, also, that they can't touch my chocolates in the fridge. As long as I do give them a lot of my one-to-one times and I am generally around, they have never resented me that time (apart from the inevitable jokes and sarcasm). So don't feel guilty, you deserve it big time. Initially, they might whine but they will settle down after they realize that you mean business. I will discuss more about this in the chapter – Care.

Touch

I am a very touchy-feely mother. I love to hug, kiss, cuddle and hold my kids. As they have grown older, I have had to hold myself back a little, especially in public. I know they might act prickly but both of them still love being hugged and kissed. In fact, my sixteen year old, very silently, will drop a kiss on my head or give me a bear hug every now and then to keep me hanging in there. And I must admit there are days when these little loving gestures energize me like nothing else! I do feel very strongly that love involves a lot of touch. That's the way we are wired. It's our social restrictions that make touch so awkward and embarrassing. I always ask young mums to hold their babies, sleep with them (makes so much sense), cuddle them, and carry them on their slings as they go on with their daily work. Don't even think of giving your babies to *dais* (midwives) for massages. Do it yourself and get the most amazing high and a deeper connect to boot! Studies have shown that touch also releases oxytocin, a nurturing chemical, into our system, which also helps in releasing milk in lactating mothers.

Playfulness quotient (PQ)

As a parent, do you feel that your day goes by leaving you completely drained?

Does life seem like an endless grind of steering your children from, 'Brush your teeth,' 'Eat your breakfast,' 'Finish your homework' or 'Get into your beds.' Has parenting become an exhausting burden for you? Do you look at your childless friends and envy their free, fun life? If your answer has been yes to most of the above questions, then there are chances that your Playfulness Quotient (PQ) is quite low.

I have to admit that this is a term I have cooked up myself (with help from my 'fun experts' – my children) as a tool to deal with the 'seriousness malaise' that seems to be hitting us parents.

It is interesting that we associate fun, friskiness and playfulness with our pre-parenting days. Once we become parents, life becomes a serious business of being responsible, dependable and taking charge. I have seen many of my friends and family lose their spark as they embrace the serious role of parenting. And the only time I do get to see their fun, playful side is when their kids are tucked into bed or visiting their grandparents.

When I ask people to list the playful activities they indulge in with their children, they talk about going to the movies, dining out or shopping. There are occasional parents who will talk about joining their children in the park or playing board games during weekends. When I talk about being playful, I mean getting in touch with the free, spontaneous child within each one of us and just having pure fun. Think about a child totally absorbed in his play. It could be just the gleeful giggling as he swings up in the air in the park, or merrily chasing the butterfly in the garden. Living totally for the moment. Extracting every bit of joy from it. I read somewhere that a forty year old laughs only four times in a day whereas a four-year-old child laughs 300 times. No laughing matter, this! I will talk more about cranking up our PQ in the chapter – Care.

As a strong campaigner for PQ (my family, friends and colleagues will vouch for ... that), I would suggest that we bring more playfulness into our life. And the best thing about being playful is that you can do it at any time of the day with your children. To understand this better, watch your little children for the next few days. It is amazing how they can bring playfulness into every aspect of their daily life. From using toothbrushes to build a car, dancing like nobody is watching, belting out Bollywood songs in the shower to building castles under the bed. Every moment is lived, explored and thoroughly enjoyed.

Deep listening and shame resilience

Kid: 'Mum, Ma'am shouted at me today though it was not my fault.'

Mum: 'I am sure you were being naughty.'

Kid: 'I don't have any friends in school. Nobody wants to play with me.'

Mum: 'If you try a little you can make friends. You don't want to try.'

Kid: 'You know what happened today?' and then begins to give a long description of some exciting news.

Dad (*peering at his laptop or the newspaper*): 'Hmm? ... Really? ... Very good!'

Why do we struggle to listen to our kids? I know I find it very challenging at times. I might be in the middle of some work, building on some thoughts, reading a book, reflecting on the so-called life-transforming ideas when suddenly the question, 'You know what happened today?' can really send me into a tailspin. Dragging myself out of my adult world with its own sense of self-importance is really a tussle. Especially when the child's demand for attention is nothing but part garbled, part silly, part fantasy of what happened in the park!

Another reason we struggle with listening is that at times it can be really painful and evoke immense anxiety. If a child complains that she has no friends in school it is easier for the parent to blame the child for not trying than to come to terms with the fact that her precious child might be very lonely or even being bullied in school.

There is no 'yes, but', 'I told you so', 'how can you', 'I think', 'why don't you' or 'at this rate' in this listening. It is about deep listening, where you just sit, absorb, contain and stay with the child. If the child brings in a little darkness, you don't try to fix it by switching on the light. You willingly sit in the dark with the child with, 'I am trying to understand how it must be for you.' It is about listening to the child from your heart without passing judgements, jumping to conclusions or trying to fix his life.

What if we could instill in our children a shame resilience that would let them sidestep shame by breaking the silence and secrecy around it? What if we could make them feel that they are worthy the way they are right now? What if we could help them grow up to be authentic and feeling comfortable in their skin about who they are? Listening is the most effective tool in helping build these attributes in our children.

You could be a parent of a teenager who has been through years of shaming that has encrusted the relationship a little. What can you do to redeem the bond again? As a parent you are carrying shame too and the best thing to do is to break the silence around it and speak up. I would suggest that to start with, it might help if you extended a direct and honest apology to your teenager. It could go like, 'I am sorry but I think I might have messed up a little when you were growing up. In my anxiety as a parent, I might have shamed you without meaning to. I am learning to build a stronger relationship with you now. I will try to bring in respect and honesty in the way I relate to you. I might still slip sometimes but do understand that I am trying. Our relationship is very precious to me and I love you so much!'

Nurturing from the heart

For me, deep listening is like the way the Na'vis greeted each other in the film *Avatar*: 'I see you'. Wow! So simple, but so difficult. In our frantic world of multitasking, who has the time for 'I see you'? But can you imagine how our lives would be transformed if we did more of 'I see you'.

Imagine a child walking into the class in the morning and the teacher doing an 'I see you' with her whole being – touch, eyes, smile and heart. Imagine each child returning home to a care-giver/parent doing an 'I see you' with her/his whole being – touch, eyes, smile and heart. And imagine each child walking through the corridors of life, classrooms of learning, sports fields of exploration, assemblies of appreciation, notice boards of creativity with an 'I see you' at every step.

To become visible, to be included, to be validated, to be welcomed, to be celebrated! Each child has a built-in dignity. It is there already, we don't have to place it there. We just have to have a little time to pause and make space for, 'I see you'. With our whole being – touch, eyes, smile and heart.

In this context I have to bring in the Nurtured Heart Approach (NHA) by Howard Glasser. A mother of a very intense child, who I had known for many years, recommended this approach to me. Prior to this, she had read piles of books, attended parenting workshops and tried medication and therapy, but nothing seemed to have worked. Finally, she started working on this approach and soon the family started noticing changes that were almost miraculous. The same family, which had come close to breaking up, having had to deal with an 'out-of-control' child, found itself experiencing intense joy and peace – feelings that had been elusive for so many years.

Over the years, I have used it with my children, in my work and my trainings. I have observed that this approach connects to everybody at a visceral level. There is always an 'aha' moment as it speaks to something deep within us. I have changed the language from the original NHA for ease of understanding and expression.

At the core of the NHA is the philosophy that there is immense inner wealth in each and every child. For many children, this inner wealth of greatness is very obvious as they shine in studies, sports, looks, talent and social situations. Like magnets, these children immediately bring out our positive energy with their charm, pleasant ways and attractive qualities. There are many other children whose greatness does not come through so easily. Their golden nuggets are buried deep in the mud and need some intentional mining in order to be extracted. They are the ones who end up attracting a lot of our negative energy as we struggle to come to terms with their 'messiness'. They seem to be grappling with their studies, are uncoordinated and have no obvious appeal, and we end up trying to fix them by directing a lot of negative energy towards them – 'you are wasting your life', 'why can't you be more responsible'!

As I had highlighted in the introduction, I find Thich Nhat Hanh's metaphor of watering the seeds very powerful. Each child has both negative seeds (anger, fear, hate, shame, rebellion) and wholesome seeds (love, joy, compassion, growth). What will blossom depends on which seeds we choose to water and nurture. That is at the core of the NHA. Greatness is a choice and our children will eventually choose greatness for themselves if we as parents choose to 'bring it into the realm of things we discern, recognize and appreciate'.

The NHA is about connecting to the greatness in each child and accepting and celebrating the child as he is. It is not a technique but a way of life. It is about loving and celebrating the child in front of you and not the child you wish he was. It is about unconditionally loving the child from your core. It requires a paradigm shift where you start valuing the worthiness of the child at a cellular level, as she is right now!

Recognitions in the NHA

Children thrive when they feel they are being appreciated, recognized and valued as human beings. In fact, that's true for all of us. However, it is also very important to differentiate between recognition and praise. Praise like 'you are so pretty', 'you are so intelligent', 'you are so smart' is like junk food, which does not really nourish a child. Carol Dweck from Stanford University, in her decade of research in this field, calls praise like 'excellent', 'very good', 'fantastic' fixed feedback (i.e., something that can't be changed), which ends up breeding a generation of praise junkies. Fixed feedback does not help the child to grow and, on the other hand, can just make her complacent and reluctant to work on her skills. However, recognitions, which highlight effort, persistence, compassion, etc., are like process feedback (i.e., something that can be changed), which enhances the growth mindset in children.

Recognition is about nourishing the heart and soul of the child with solid nutritious food.

So how does it play out in our day-to-day life? How can we learn to be mindful of our daily interactions with our children and start vitalizing them with a regular dose of recognition.

Let's go through the various types of recognitions as explained by the NHA:

Active recognition

Active recognition is the 'I see you' of the Na'vis. I like to believe that my grandfather was a Na'vi, at least for his grandchildren. It seemed as if he relished every moment of our being on this earth. He was very quietly aware of whatever we were doing. No matter how busy he was, or how many times he had seen us in a day, he would always smile when we entered the room, his eyes lighting up and sparkling with pure love. As he grew very old, at times, we could hear him softly chuckling and murmuring our names under his breath as if just saying them gave him immense pleasure and peace. That is active recognition! When just the presence of the other person fills you with immense gratitude and joy.

Many times, after a day's work, I would enter home, still a little preoccupied with my to-do list, to catch a quick hug, kiss and a distracted, 'How was your day, sweetie?' Now after some soul searching, I do more of the 'lighting up' whenever I meet my kids. I am ready to leave whatever I am thinking or doing and smile, with all my love showing in my eyes. This is a small gesture but it works like magic in building a sense of 'I am valued' for children and gives me a big shot of love and warmth!

Children flourish when they receive a steady dose of active recognition and light up. It could be in the form of eye contact, touch, their name being called out or just acknowledging what they are doing.

'I see you are reading a book.'

'What are you drawing?'

'You are having your milk,' etc.

In our distracted world, where we are multitasking all the time, active recognition makes the child feel more visible, feel wanted. If you have noticed there is no praise in active recognition, just appreciation of the presence. Simple.

Active recognition also includes picking up feelings and acknowledging them. 'Are you sad about not doing well in your test?' I can make out that you are a little angry with your brother. Am I right?' Active recognition is about listening, looking, touching and feeling. It is about receiving the child in your world with all senses.

Reflection – 'Light up'

Choose one day and make it an active recognition day. Go about your daily activities but keep your eyes and ears open for your children. Look at them more often, make more eye contact, listen to them, touch them, smile at them, light up and notice the small activities they are involved in (tone it down for the teenagers otherwise you might spook them out). At the end of the day, just notice if you see any changes in them, or in yourself. For that little extra kick, try it with your spouse too!

Value recognition

In value recognition, we go one step further. We connect their behaviour, actions, choices to a strength, a quality or a value. 'I appreciate your honesty in telling me that you did not prepare for your exams.'

'It takes a lot of courage to stand up to the bullies.'

'You showed a sense of responsibility in submitting this project on time.'

From a very young age, children hear stories about themselves that have words like 'smart', 'intelligent', 'naughty', 'talkative', 'slow' or 'lazy'. They make the most of these words to build their own narratives which they might carry for the rest of their lives.

In value recognition, we become active agents in

extracting the threads of these narratives and highlighting them through language. By acknowledging them, we make them come alive. We help children in weaving their unique identity with vibrant and colourful threads that speak to them of their worthiness and growth. Value recognition connects the acknowledgement to specific behaviour. It is different from vague approval like, 'You are so smart', or 'You are so confident'. Children sense the phoniness of this cheerleading that we all can get into – 'Wow', 'Amazing', 'Super', 'Brilliant', 'Excellent'. Sounds great but does not do much in building their sense of worth or growth mindset.

You might wonder if you could do it with little children, as their vocabularies are so limited. However, you might be surprised at how quickly they pick up the words and make it part of their vocabulary too. I remember when my kids were little I started this game which they loved. Every time they did something positive that needed attention, I would acknowledge it on our big white board. Suppose my son had been considerate to my daughter, I would write down the word on the board and it used to be fun listening to him decode it and add it to his vocabulary.

The most important thing to keep in mind here is that recognition is not to be confused with praise, pep talk or sugar coating. It is a genuine expression of appreciation of their skills, qualities, abilities, strengths, assets and affinities as they are growing and building their sense of self.

Reflection

Every time you see your child doing something positive – call it something. Start building your vocabulary to include a range of playful, creative and different adjectives. Do not just settle for 'good', 'well done', and 'excellent'. Start talking about how they are being responsible, organized, compassionate, articulate, assertive, courageous, hard-working, persistent, adventurous, independent, alert, curious, determined, forgiving, generous, helpful, inclusive, kind, loving, patient, sensitive and strong. Start highlighting their leadership skills, sense of justice, out-of-the-box thinking, friendship skills, sense of aesthetics, passion for wild life, calmness, confidence and the ability to stand up for others. Start watering these seeds of traits, qualities, abilities and skills you want to build in them. It is best to start as early as possible to identify and nurture them, and let them hone them.

Exception recognition

Whatever difficulty you might be facing with your child, there will be times when the exceptions are happening. Start looking out for those little windows. So, for example, if you are upset with your husband every time he flings the wet towel on the bed, you might start noticing the times when he is actually putting the towel out to dry. You might let him know that you appreciated his thoughtfulness (without a hint of sarcasm).

My daughter likes to draw, cut, paste, scribble, strum, nibble, ride a ripstick, chat, read and all of this at the same time. All this can lead to a lot of mess. I found that rather than always pointing out the clutter to her, it was more effective when I noticed the times she was being organized. So very soon, she would clear up after her and then check with me, 'Do you think I am being organized?'

Similarly, for a child who gets angry easily, you might notice the times he stayed calm. For another child who puts off doing homework, you could mention the times he came to the study table without whining too much. If your child is a little anxious you could point out the time she spoke up in front of others. You could put it across as, 'I know how anger/procrastination/fears troubles you at times but I saw the way you handled it now. I think it takes courage to do that.'

So proactive recognition overlaps with strength recognition but the difference is that we are looking at the exceptions the child is making in learning a skill or managing a difficulty and we recognize it.

Children like to be noticed when they are trying. They give up trying when they feel it is being ignored. So recognize the smallest step they are taking.

Creative recognition

Some children are very visible and recognitions like pretty, intelligent, talented, responsible, hard-working and creative flow easily for them. Being pretty, intelligent or creative comes much more naturally to them. Going back to the core philosophy that, 'Each child is wired and inspired differently', we have to accept that there are many children who do not possess these socially desirable traits. They are shy, scattered, disorganized, dreamers, clumsy and noisy. They might still have huge reservoirs of creativity, talent, ability, generosity, etc., but all that is lost behind cobwebs of miswiring that keep them from connecting and showing their sparkle.

Creative recognition is about creating spaces for all children to shine. It is about making time for each child to be celebrated. My daughter called me very excitedly at work one day after returning from school. She declared that she had been awarded a certificate by her class: a Dynamic Dynamite Award! It read, 'This award is presented to Anya Sen for being "The Florence Nightingale, with Slash (lead guitarist of Guns 'N' Roses) in her fingers".' The best part was that each child in the class had been awarded a certificate ranging from the 'Bhaag Milkha Bhaag' and 'Zen Master of Our Class' to the 'Original Benjamin' and 'Roald Dahl' award. They had even invited the school's director, principal and vice-principal for the little ceremony.

I believe that we make stories and stories make us. Also, our stories are not actually stories until they have found an audience. In our narrative therapy language, we call these the definitional ceremonies, which rejoice and applaud the rich stories that have been forgotten or neglected by society. Just a little ceremony, which, I am sure, the kids are going to cherish for the rest of their lives.

I wish we could stretch ourselves a little and do these

ceremonies for all our children. Raghav's poem to be read out to the class; Rhea's story to be sent to the school magazine; Sahil's artwork to be put up on the noticeboard; Shreya's painting to be framed at home and put up in the living room; Ananya's recipe to be put up on a children's website. Let them make their own blogs, encourage them for show and tell activities, let them participate more in assemblies, and sports and annual days. Let childhood and school not be congratulatory just for children who are visible to all, but also for those who are not, who can easily get lost in the crowd. Another form of 'I see you' of the Na'vis.

Three Stands of NHA

At the heart of the NHA are three stands, three principles that guide and give shape to this whole approach:

Stand 1: Relentlessly energize positivity. If we see our attention, eye contact, words and body language as energy we invest in others then this stand is about persistently watering the wholesome seeds in our children. For example, every time I see my daughter making 'on-track choices', I spot those and recognize them through eye contact, a smile, a touch and strength recognition.

Stand 2: Refuse to energize negativity. If I see my daughter making some 'off-track choices', like being rude or not using kind words, I remove the energy. I do not give in to energizing her negative choices. This one is tougher than stand one as we are so used to picking up and highlighting everything that is going wrong – 'stop talking rudely', 'look at the mess you have made here', or 'you have to learn to be more organized'. Somewhere, we feel, by highlighting and talking about it, immediately the child would understand her mistake and not do it again. This does not work! But we still keep doing it just as our parents did with us and their parents did with them.

Stand 3: Mindful reset. Get back on track whenever we feel ourselves leak negatively. This one is again very difficult. Do you remember the last time you realized that you were getting cranky, irritable, angry, unreasonable, demanding or difficult? How easy was snapping out of it? Negativity is so sticky, it's tough to shake it off. And most of us are not even aware that we are getting into the negativity loop. So for me, mindful reset is about resetting myself before the 'cranky mum' really takes over. Firstly, it is about using our 'parental mindful meter' to track our feelings and thought patterns through the day. Secondly, it is about catching ourselves at the right time before we lose ourselves to negativity. Thirdly, it is about taking a deep breath, breathing out of the negativity loop and resetting to a higher level or a better version of ourselves.

I have a simple ABCDE formula that can explain this better. Do remember this formula as it might feature later (I use it flexibly in many situations):

A: Alertness to any negativity – This is about keeping the

parental mindful meter on and sensing immediately when you find yourself sinking deeper and deeper into negativity. You might feel irritable, snappy, caught into blaming, shaming or complaining.

B: Breathing – Focus on your breathing, deep and slow, and just let your body relax for a moment or two.

C: Change the channel (Kids love this bit!) – Just like you immediately change the channel on your TV when something terrible is showing, you change the channel of your mind. Gently amp up your feelings to a joyful state by bringing to your mind all the things that make you happy. If there are residual feelings of irritation or worry, don't fight them; just let them be there without watering them.

D: Do something else – Just moving your body can change your energy levels. Stretch your body, if possible go for a little walk, do a funny little jig, walk out to the balcony and breathe in some fresh air.

E: Energize yourself by doing something playful – Smile, laugh, giggle, sing and dance and you will immediately reset yourself to a happier, joyous and peaceful self.

Create their memory box
Get a big box and cover it with your child's drawings and sketches. If required do some cut outs, add photographs of some of their favourite characters, for e.g., someone from

Harry Potter, Star Wars, Lord of the Rings or Spiderman.
Start putting together a collection of their little 'victories'.
Their hand prints (I am sure you have them tucked away
somewhere), their first word on a post-it, CDs of their dance
performances, their paintings from pre-school, some valued
certificates, little colourful notes of what teachers, family or
friends might have said about them (only celebratory things
go into the box). Photocopies of their school magazine
articles, pictures of them playing the guitar, drawing,
dancing, cycling, climbing trees, mountain-trekking, taking
care of the neighbourhood puppies. A good idea is to put
one 'celebration' from each stage of their life. To make it
meaningful for them, let it be symbolic of who they are as
human beings rather than just a collection of odds and ends.
It might become a little worn down and tattered (make sure
you get a good quality box), but I can assure you that it will be
one of their most prized possessions for the rest of their life!

Building richer narratives

We create stories and stories create us. From the time our
children are small, we start making stories about them. 'She
is so smart, I am sure she will grow up to be a doctor.' 'He is
so stubborn, he will have problems making friends.' 'She is so
good at art, I am sure she will grow to be very artistic.' These
stories are being churned out every moment, every hour,
every day and every week. Children start living these stories as
naturally as they carry their names. 'I am smart, so I will be a
doctor.' 'I am artistic.' 'I am stubborn so I can't make friends.'

Sometimes these stories are rich and varied like colours

of the rainbow. When I meet parents for the first time, I like to ask them to describe what they value most about their children. There are some parents who go into an instant high – their eyes start sparkling, they laugh, they chuckle, they glow, tripping on their words to describe every unique, endearing quality of their precious one. They might talk about how he is so loving, so sensitive, so curious, so creative, such an out-of-the-box thinker, and the stories flow on and on. Never mind that just five minutes back they had been in a bind with tears in their eyes, describing how the same precious one had been giving them sleepless nights. Actually, that's what makes it even more heartwarming.

Then there are parents who actually respond to this question with a startled 'What?' They look at each other questioningly, wondering if they are at the right place with the right person. I do empathize with their confusion as obviously they have all been prepared with a long list of problems, challenges, difficulties that they have scribbled furiously in their diaries. However, after some time, when they realize that I am serious, they stutter with, 'We can't really think of any. He used to be good at cricket but he has stopped playing now,' or maybe 'He plays the guitar very well, but that is not going to take him far in life, is it?'

My heart goes out to these parents (don't even get me started on children) on how painful and burdensome their lives must be that they couldn't find anything that they value in their child.

More than how we talk to our children, we need to think about how we talk about them.

Think of our children's childhood memories as albums they carry with them for their life. Every day, we are helping them to add different pictures to this album. There might be some pictures which are discoloured, black and white, maybe a little torn or crumpled. However, as long as they are small and spaced out among many colourful, vibrant, lively and joyful pictures – this album will nourish them for life.

Reflection

Reflect on some stories you might be holding about your children. How do you describe your children to other people? As parents, what language do you use when you are talking about your children? When you are thinking about your children, what are the repeated themes that come up?

Are these stories very sparse, thin, unidimensional?
'He is just so lazy.'
    'She always wants her way.'
    'He wants to waste his life.'

Do you have to struggle to think of anything positive? Does this reflection fill you with a sense of heaviness? Or are these stories rich, varied and full of energy?
'He is such a dreamer.'

'She knows her mind.'
'He is taking his time to explore life.'

Do these stories come out easily? Along with the exasperated sigh is there a smile and a sense of wonder too? Do you talk about their early years to them? What is the flavour of these telling and retelling of stories? What pictures are you helping your child to add to his album every day?

Have you noticed how children love hearing stories about their early years? They hang on to every word you utter as you tell them about the time when they were born, how they cried, how they slept (or didn't!), what they liked to eat, their first words, their first steps, their first day in school, lullabies, bedtime stories, songs, toys, their antics, quirks, oddities and fancies. All laid out like a collage of multiple hues. These are stories that are told and retold till they acquire a life of their own.

'Tell me again how I used to act like Tarzan?'

'Tell me, how did you feel when they told you that you had given birth to a girl?'

I love discussing these memories with my children. They always give me such a sense of wonder, humour, warmth and a wonderful dose of GEMS – genuine emotional moments – as one of my friend calls it. Remember the last time you suddenly chanced upon an old photo of your child when he was a baby when you were clearing up some shelves? Just the thought of it will make you feel warm and bring a big smile to your face.

Connect is the essence of parenting. It is the foundation and core of your relationship with your child. Though I have tried to explain some techniques, please remember they are not Connect, just some ways to reach it. Connect comes from the heart and not from the brain. It is like an invisible cord from your heart to your child's. At times this cord is throbbing with pulsating energy and vitality and there might be times when it seems a little shrivelled, weak and dried-up. Our role as parents is to do whatever we can to pump in radiant light, positive energy, love and joy into the cord.

Each child carries a rainbow. We are like prisms that have to catch their light and bring their unique rainbow into life.

2

COACH –
BUILDING LIFE
SKILLS

'Problems cannot be solved at the level they were created.'

—Albert Einstein

*W*e all want our children to excel, do well in studies, be physically fit and active, socialize (and be popular!), listen to us, be respectful, be responsible, be independent, be organized, manage their time well, value money, not be angry or rude or scared, be confident, be happy and do all this as quickly as possible!

A tall order indeed! If anybody demanded this from us as adults we would be shocked but we do not even bat an eyelid while expecting this from our children. These are the dreams we have been carrying for them. They are there, deep down – expecting, measuring, demanding. We measure our worth according to how well the children fit into those dreams. If they fall short, we feel cheated, angry, depressed and wonder 'Why me?' We feel inadequate and, in our anxiety, react by cranking up our resentment towards our children. We become judgemental, critical and comparative. And, therefore, get stuck in a spiral of negativity. Before we know it, unhealthy patterns of a lifetime get carved out.

I am going to borrow from the famous psychotherapist Eric Berne's Transactional Analysis (TA), a method of studying interactions between people, to illustrate this concept a little more. Berne started TA and it became quite a rage in the 1970s. It is not so popular any more, but I am going to use one of its concepts, as it is very accessible and effective. I will give you just the simplified version. According to the TA, each of us constantly operates through one of these three states at any given time: Parent – Critical and Nurturing (CP and NP), Adult (A) and a Child – Free Child and Rebellious Child (FC and RC). These terms do not necessarily correspond to their common definitions as used in the English language.

So, for example, if I see my daughter eating junk food, my Critical Parent (CP) might come out and say, 'I am sick and tired of all that rubbish you eat. Why can't you eat more fruits?' I might come from my Nurturing Parent (NP) and say, 'Are you hungry, sweety? Can I make you something yummy to eat?' I could be an all Adult (A) – rational, logical, non-emotional, clear-thinking brain and sit down and tell her the effect consuming that bag of chips would have on her health. I could also be Rebellious Child (RC) and snatch it from her and shout, 'I won't give it, what will you do?' Or I could just be a Free Child (FC) and say, 'Yummy, please, can I have some of those too?'

Some transactions become more entrenched into unhealthy patterns. One such crucial transaction that I would like to highlight here is between your Critical Parent (CP) and your Rebellious Child (RC). So, going back to the example of my daughter and her bag of chips, she might react to my Critical Parent's, 'I am sick and tired of all that rubbish you eat. Why can't you eat more fruits?' by saying 'There is nothing to eat in this house except for those stale apples and I hate them!' I would react to that statement by

Figure 2.1 Eric Berne's Transactional Analysis

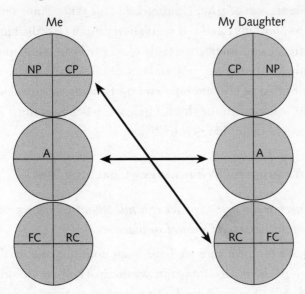

cranking up my CP quotient, 'If you had bothered to open the fridge then you would have found the lovely salad that I made for you. You are so lazy!' This would boost her RC quotient more and she would just get up and walk off. At this point, the feedback loop would begin to go round and round. In the end, we would have one angry, frustrated parent and an equally angry, rebellious child who wants to shut herself up in her room. If we are honest, then we can all admit we have been there sometimes and it is not a good feeling.

In this chapter, we are going to look at how we can help our children become more responsible without getting caught in that negativity rut. A long time back I came across this book titled, *Stop Parenting, Start Coaching* and I really loved the title. It resonated so deeply with my belief that our role as parents is to help our children build life skills. Some skills like responsibility and self-regulation cannot be drilled into children using ineffective tools like criticism, complaints, blaming, shaming, nagging and lectures. They all come from the position of CP and only end up hooking or provoking the RC quotient of the child. There will be no learning if we are caught up in that negativity loop.

Pre-requisites: What Makes Coaching Work?

Connect as the first step: We can talk about Coaching only if we have a strong Connect in place.

We have to make sure we have made solid deposits in the emotional bank account before we think of helping children build skills. For example, let's say you are concerned about how little exercise your child is getting. If your Connect is not so strong at the time (you might have been busy at work, preoccupied with a new project, etc.), chances are high that when you do bring up the topic, the child might react by getting angry and expressing resentment. That would immediately hook your CP quotient and both of you would be caught up in the negativity loop. On the other hand, if your Connect has been strong where you have enjoyed spending time with him and there has been an easy flow of positive energy between the two of you, then chances are high that when you do bring up the topic in question, he might not react and actually listen to you.

Empathy and compassion

Many times, as parents, we get lost in the behaviour of the child: 'He is so rude to me.' 'He is constantly fighting with his sister.' 'There are too many complaints about him from school'.

A very important element of coaching is to move beyond behaviour and understand the emotions.

What is he feeling right now? If we stay locked into overt behaviour we lose the chance of connecting to the powerful emotions behind the behaviour that might be stopping the child from making the right choice. For example, if the child is extremely sullen and rude after returning from school, it might be helpful for you to find out what is making him so upset rather than chastizing him for his rudeness. He is probably being bullied or struggling socially. It is only when you have connected to the emotions that you can bring about a change.

The main goal of coaching is moving the child from RC to Adult. Adult is the clear thinking, logical and reasonable part of us. CP feeds and pumps up the RC and shrinks the Adult. Only your Adult or even NP can connect to the child's Adult. I have found that the best way for me to connect to the child's Adult is by first using my NP to listen to him, empathize and connect to his emotions. If he did feel that you had heard him out and understood his emotions, then it is easy to move to my Adult and engage his Adult. I like to use the 'You, Me and We Approach' to hook on to the child's Adult.

This approach follows these three steps:
- Listen to his point of view first
- Bring up your thoughts about it
- Arrive at a solution together

Consider a scenario where the mother is concerned that the child is not getting enough exercise:

Mum: 'Hi, how was your day in school?'

As the Connect is strong, the mother's question would not be seen as a threat or intrusion but as a genuine need to connect.

Shiv: 'Usual …' (*highlights some bits*).

Mum takes interest in what Shiv has to share and listens without interrupting. Then she asks him if it is okay to discuss something with him.

Mum: 'Please help me understand why you have stopped going to the park in the evening?'

If Shiv does not feel threatened and he does not feel that a lecture is soon coming his way, then there are strong chances that he might be honest and straightforward in giving the answer.

Shiv: 'Umm … I don't know. I do not really have time … There is so much to do.'

Rather than jumping into 'Of course, you have the time if you cut down on your TV!', mum listens to him and empathizes.

Mum: 'I know the feeling. I really struggle with the same. I find it helpful to start with just fifteen minutes in a day and then slowly build it up. What do you think we need to do to get you to find that time?'

Half the battle is won if children feel that the parents understand and empathize. We spend too much time telling children how flawless, strong, hard-working and perfect we are. If instead, we let them see our vulnerabilities and imperfections (judiciously, according to their age), they are much more open to us. If Shiv knows that his mother has the same struggles but she still persists, he might be more open to suggestions for changes in his routine to accommodate exercises. I have shared how I struggled with shyness most of my life and how I was easily intimidated by some people with my children. They see these vulnerabilities and see how I still persist despite them.

Honour

We need to honour our children at all times no matter what their behaviour is. When I say that it does not mean we shrug off all our responsibilities and let them do and behave as they please. I mean that no matter what the situation, whether he has been rude, hit his brother, broken a rule, got a detention from school, we will continue to honour the child. We learn to separate the child from his behaviour and the message we give is, 'I love you and honour you, but I am not all right about the behaviour and we need to find out a way to address this.'

This can be a very powerful approach in helping the children understand boundaries and consequences without losing their sense of self-worth.

Let's imagine a situation where you were getting late to work every day and your boss called you to her office. Would you feel more empowered to come in early if you were shouted at and shamed, or if it was discussed with you respectfully and a solution arrived at after your problem had been heard?

ZPD

The concept of Zone of Proximal Development (ZPD) was developed by the well-known Russian educational psychologist, Lev Vygotsky. According to Vygotsky, ZPD means that as far as different skills are concerned, we all fall somewhere on a continuum. For example, on a scale of 0–10, I might fall at 3 in my math skills; 9 in my reading skills; 4 in my cooking skills; 6 in my baking skills; 5 in my dancing skills (though 10 in passion for dancing); 7 in my climbing skills; 2 in my running skills; and 8 in my playfulness skills. These numbers are my ZPD in different skills. Each one of us has a profile with hues of different colours that makes us who we are. However, the interesting thing about ZPD is that it is not static; it can change. There is a mantra in neurosciences, 'Use it or lose it'. What it means is that our brain is like a muscle, the more we use certain parts of it the more it develops. It is a continuous process. So, if you had met me when I was in school or college, my ZPD in time management and organizational skills was around 3. Now on good days I can stretch it up to 6 or even 7. It has come with a lot of practice, training and conscious effort. Before we start coaching a child in any skill, it is important that we find out what his ZPD is in that area.

Acceptance

My fascination for neurosciences has made me understand one thing – each child is wired differently and it is extremely important that we learn to respect that. If we take different skills like reading, writing, playing football, dancing, time management or anger management, each child's ZPD can be put somewhere or the other in the continuum for each. It is part of their wiring.

There is a difference when we view the child as being lazy, irresponsible, sloppy, clumsy, dull and cranky, or when we accept, maybe, that his skills in this particular area are low. The former comes from a place of judgement whereas the latter comes from simple acceptance.

If you are concerned about how untidy your child's room is, rather than calling her messy or dirty, it might be more helpful to accept that maybe her organizational skills are not that well developed yet. Her ZPD in that area is likely to be around 3. If children feel judged (the CP scenario), then they react (the RC quotient cranking up). However, if you come from the place of acceptance (A), they might respond by being more understanding and willing to work on it.

Do remember, many times wiring is very much heritable. So, if you have always struggled with managing your time, then chances of your children having similar traits are higher. Therefore, before you judge them (Believe me, it is so much easier to judge kids than look within!), reflect on your own wiring. Do you have similar difficulties, or maybe you had them but you have trained yourself over time to become more organized.

Step-by-step coaching

Therefore Coaching does not mean we give up and say, 'That's what she was born with and that's where she will stay.' Start with the skill that you feel your child needs to work on and break it into small easy steps. Get down to the level of ZPD she is at and start building it up gradually. If she is at 3 and you expect her to be at 7, then there is going to be a lot of frustration and conflict and not much of learning. For example, if you want your child to become more independent in getting ready for school, make a list of the things she needs to do the previous night and in the morning. Break the list up into a daily drill checklist for each chunk: bag, uniform, bathroom and breakfast. Put it up on the noticeboard or bathroom mirror and supervise at each step in the beginning until she becomes more confident. You can step back from the day she begins to do everything on her own. Recognize her for every bit of effort she put towards the right direction.

Have you ever been curious to know how killer whales in sea life parks are trained to jump over a four-feet-high rope? You might think that they start with giving the whales rewards after every little jump and slowly increase the height of the rope? Wrong! They start by first laying down the rope on the pool floor and every time the whale swims across it they reward the mammal. Slowly and gradually, they string the rope higher and higher! I think it is a beautiful metaphor for Coaching: there is nothing like too low or too slow!

Hands on

A Coach is like a warrior who has to be out in the arena, giving all her time, energy, love and loads of patience. She has to roll up her sleeves, get her hands dirty, be on the floor and sweat it out till she is ready to hit the bed. There is no other way. Shouting out orders from the benches will not work. She will only end up with a sore throat, frustration and a 'they refuse to listen to me' defeatist attitude. You need to communicate your instructions effectively. Get down to their eye level, maintain eye contact and speak clearly and confidently. Touch them gently to make sure you have their full attention.

I do joke about how my work really starts when I reach home. There are days when I would love to go home and not talk to anybody but just find a quiet corner where I could burrow myself underneath my covers with my book. Delicious thought but best to let it go.

Listening to their chatter about their day, negotiating through their requests, dodging their nagging (kids nag and how!), keeping an eagle eye for overuse of screen time, getting homework done, making sure they clear up after them, saying no for all snacks before dinner, organizing dinner, making sure they eat that dinner, planning their next day's football class, making sure they take their bath, get to bed on time, read a little, switch off the light at the right time with a cuddle, a kiss and 'love you'. Phew! Being a parent is like being a warrior. We are living a warrior's life!

Surrogate frontal lobe

Our frontal lobe is the conductor of the orchestra, i.e., our brain. It makes sure that all the circuits are moving in coordination so that the symphony of daily activities is smooth. So whether you are driving home from work, cooking the evening meal or working on a project, it makes sure that all parts of the brain work effectively together. The main 'executive' functions of the frontal lobe are attention, sustained attention, inhibitory control (won't have chocolate as I am on a diet), working memory (mental notepad or RAM of a computer), emotional regulation (I am going to stay calm and not get angry), time management and organization skills.

If I could draw parallels, I would equate the frontal lobe to the 'Adult' of the TA model. The calm, rational, clear thinking part of us. We all want our children to have a well-developed frontal lobe or 'Adult'. If you pick up books on success (for example, *Seven Habits of Highly Effective People*), you will find that the core skills mentioned have everything to do with the frontal lobe 'executive' skills or the Adult.

The frontal lobes of children are a work in progress. Brains develop from back to front so the frontal lobe is the last to develop by the time the individual is around twenty-one years of age. Even during this growing and fine-tuning period, each child's frontal lobe develops at a different rate. Some are early bloomers and some bloom late in life.

So, what can parents do to build those skills in children? If you get emotional, it immediately hooks the emotional brain (limbic system) of the child and not the frontal lobe. As explained earlier, the best way to hook/train the frontal lobe (Adult) of the child is if the parent uses his frontal lobe (Adult).

Sometimes parents have to step in as 'surrogate' frontal lobes for their children when they find that their children are unable to use their frontal lobes effectively.

For example, if your child is struggling with time management then, rather than criticizing him (which will only hook his CP), you could work with him by helping him work out his schedule for exams or project submission. You could step in as a reminder for the tasks he needs to do on a daily basis. Similarly, for a child who has anger management issues, you could help him calm down and, then, later, when he is calmer, think of some strategies he can use to look out for early triggers of anger and how to stay cool no matter what the provocation.

Inside-out approach

The mantra is, 'The only person I can change is myself.'

So, no matter what the situation, rather than blaming the child or finding fault with him, you look within. 'What am I feeling right now?'

'Am I doing the best I can as a parent?'

'What do I need to do?'

For example, your child comes back from school very upset as he has scored very low marks in his exam. Do you get on the fault-finding, shame-inducing mode, criticizing him for not studying enough and peppering it with a few 'I told you so's?' Or do you become mindful of the intense anxiety within you, slowly let it go and then reflect on 'What do I need to do?' The answer might be as simple as 'Just listen to him right now.' Or let's say, your child has become very rude and irritable lately. You could either react or get angry with her or you could reflect on, 'I wonder why she has been so irritable and rude these days? How have I been at home recently? I know I have been stressed with work and I have been snapping at her.' So, no matter what the situation, you look within and reflect on your own feelings and your action plan as a parent.

A reactive approach makes us assume the position of a victim.

'Why me?'

'Why do my children have to behave like this?'

'Why can't my children be as smart as other children?'

'Why am I so unlucky?'

The inside-out approach helps us assume a more empowered position: 'My child is struggling in school right now, what do I need to do as a parent?' I have found this approach very empowering as it cuts down on helplessness and makes me feel that there is always something I can do as a parent.

Many a times, our children's struggles reflect those of our own. After all, they have inherited our genes and wiring. So, if I struggle with time management, my children might too. Partly due to their wiring and partly due to what they have seen me do. If, as a parent, I have not understood and reflected on this, I might feel extremely flustered about it as watching their struggles presses all the panic buttons in me. Therefore that self-awareness is extremely important to help me maintain the reflective, inside-out approach.

Do something different

> 'Insanity is doing something again and again and expecting different results.'
>
> —Albert Einstein, physicist

If this quote is true, then all parents are insane! Many times I hear parents complain, 'Every day I have to shout at him in the morning and only then will he get ready on time. Why does he not change despite my saying the same thing again and again?' Good question! He is not going to change till the time parents decide to change. We nag, lecture, criticize, complain and shout as we want the child to change and when he does not, we keep amping it up slowly and steadily till it becomes unbearable for everyone. Many times I catch myself saying something I know is not going to bring about any change at all, 'I am tired of saying this every day, but why can't you please pack up your bag after finishing homework?' or 'How many times do I have to tell you to brush your teeth before sleeping?'

'Do something different' is a simple solution to a lot of our problems, but we rarely want to try it as we get stuck in unhealthy patterns of behaviours or habits. We are too lazy to try anything different.

Sometime ago, I was working with the family of a child with Attention Deficit Hyperactivity Disorder (ADHD). The parents were very concerned about some of his 'out-of-control' behaviours. For example, every day, when he would come back from school, he would throw a huge tantrum, shouting, screaming, hitting and biting. For many months, the parents had been trying to control this behaviour by cajoling him, requesting him, bribing him, even shouting and, at times, hitting him, but nothing seemed to be working. I suggested to them that maybe they could do something really different that would break the pattern. I did emphasize that they would have to think of something so bizarre that it would stop the tantrum on its track. The parents, desperate to try anything (and somewhat used to my whacky ideas), agreed and went home. So the very next day, as expected, as soon as the child reached home and started to throw a tantrum, the mother suddenly dived under the dining table. The child, suddenly finding the sole audience missing, stopped mid-tantrum and peered under the table to find his mother sitting calmly. Immediately, thinking it was a new game, he dived under the table too and soon the mother had him rolling on the floor giggling and laughing as she tickled him. When they came back to me they had some interesting stories about how they managed to control the after-school tantrum.

Some of you might be a little alarmed at this approach, calling it too bizarre and weird but I can tell you it works like magic. So, the next time your child refuses to go to sleep, take a bath, brush his teeth or wear his clothes, I would suggest that you do something really bizarre and crazy and see how he responds.

Creativity and play

I have already, hopefully, made a very strong case for notching up our PQ with our children in the previous chapter.

Playfulness is one of the most essential ingredients of our relationship with children. Kids respond best to play. Words, orders, reminders, instructions, 'have to', 'should' or 'must' do not make sense to them at times. Bring play, laughter, silliness, song, dance, colour, fun, imagination and fantasy into their lives and see them come alive. The dreary day-to-day activities that can become such a drag sometimes will become a breeze if we boost them with play. So brushing teeth could be about declaring war on the germs with its artillery, a war song ending with a 'yoohoo' of victory. Colouring could be about feeding different colours to the hungry flowers who shout out 'thank you'. Homework time could be about having an imaginary classroom with your child taking responsibility for being the monitor and making sure everybody did his or her work. My son used to love this game when he was little. He would be very excited about raising his hand and giving the right answer and being told that he was my 'star student'. He would do his work with enthusiasm and make sure others finished theirs too!

I know some of you might think it is too silly or that the children can become used to this and not do things just because they need to be done. Well that stage will also arrive one day as they grow older and independent. However, I would strongly suggest that if you are struggling with one aspect of parenting, infuse it with playfulness and see the change. I know this requires a lot of effort (though it can be equally energizing too) and innovativeness, but, maybe, to start with, choose one area that you would want to address first.

I remember when my kids were little, I used to find myself

becoming a little tired, irritable and cranky at the end of the day, especially around their bath time. To make it more fun, I decided that I would use that time to sing to my kids or tell them stories. There was an immediate transformation as bath times became something we started looking forward to.

It is important to highlight that no one strategy works forever with children. We have to keep it varied, keep changing the tricks, find new twists to the games and new moves to keep them interested and enthusiastic. So keep playing, innovating, inventing, discovering and fantasizing. There is no limit to creativity.

Seven Steps to Highly-effective Coaching

Clear goal

'What is the one skill I want to nurture in my child which will help her become a more healthy, responsible, independent and happy human being?'

Depending on the age of the child, it could range from eating well, sleeping on her own, staying fit, doing less screen, being more organized, managing time better, being financially savvy, getting better grades, being more communicative, articulate, confident, happy, sociable, respectful, emotionally balanced, focused and so on and so forth. We would all like that in our children. It makes our work easier as parents and feels good to boot. However, just start with one or two skills. Make it very specific. Rather than making good habits a goal as it is too vague, be more specific and narrow it down to one or, maybe, two activities.

For example, clear up the bathroom after using it or go and play in the park every day.

Rate it on a scale of 0 to 10 where 5 is in the middle

a. 'Where is my child right now in that skill?'
b. 'Where does he need to be?'
c. 'What is the one step he needs to take that will help him move one point up in that scale?'
d. 'What would I need to do to help him move one step further?'

These are extremely important questions as they help you identify the ZPD of the child, clarify the goal and establish the next step forward, for you and for your child. For example, you want your child to get better grades. You might identify that on the scale he is at 3 where the goal is 8. I would always suggest that you stay away from making 10 as a goal as it will then make you seek perfection (which I think is a huge problem) and establish extremely high expectations (for a child who is at 3 right now). The next step that you might think would work in helping him move to 4 would be to make him sit down and study for an extra half hour every day. You might want to keep yourself free around that time so that you could provide him some level of 'scaffolding' till he is ready to sit and work on his own.

Ask instead of telling

We are constantly telling children what they need to do and not ask them as much as is required what they would want to do. (I had highlighted in the previous chapter that 'kids will do well if they can'.) So, you could sit down with your child and ask, 'Are you happy with your grades right now?' Make sure you ask without sounding sarcastic or angry.

'Do you think you are putting in enough time?'

'On a scale of 0 to 10, where are you right now?'

'Where would you like to be?'

'What is the next step you need to take to move up one step?'

'How can I help you in this?'

You will realize that all these questions are reflective and it is your Adult that is engaging the child's Adult. One of the main goals of parenting and of growing up is building that Adult in your child. As we have discussed before, that Adult cannot be nurtured by your CP. You have to genuinely get into your Adult to do so. The reason I am using the word genuine so many times is because you might think you are in your Adult but actually it is your CP speaking. The best way to check if you are in your CP or your Adult is to ask yourself these questions:

'Am I feeling calm or are there traces of anger, resentment, irritation or annoyance?'

'Am I genuinely trying to ask and listen to the answer or do I want to prove a point right now?'

'Will I continue to stay calm even if he does not give the right answers?'

You will be amazed how well children respond to this approach.

Draw up a plan

For any change to happen you would have to get down and draw up a clear plan. So carrying on with the same example, you might want to first make sure that your connect with your child is solid and strong (I cannot emphasize that enough). Then you might want to sit with him and ask him a few questions regarding how he feels about his grades. You could take a *'You, Me, We Approach'* that I highlighted earlier. Chances are high that if you have a strong connect and you are coming from your Adult, then he could respond from his Adult too rather than his RC. Initially, he might show a bit of his RC (I hate studying, it is so boring); listen to him, empathize with it (I know it can be a drag sometimes. I remember feeling like that), but bring him back to the issue (I can understand you find it boring but we still need to do it). After being listened to and understanding your point of view, he might agree that he needs to work on his grades too. That's when you need to gently work out a plan of action. Make sure you don't make it too overwhelming and remember he is at 3 and we just want him to move up to 4 and not 8. Work out when he could take out that hour for studying, where he would like to study, with whom, how, etc.

Rhythms and routines

When we lived in England, I heard a very experienced nanny say once, 'There is nothing like a bad child, there are just bad routines!' It sounds a bit drastic but there is a lot of truth in that statement. I do believe that if children follow a clear routine then you have already won half the battle (actually there might not be much of a battle). Routines give a rhythm and flow to the day. If a child knows that after school she can relax for an hour followed by homework time at 4 p.m., playtime from 5 to 7 p.m. and then bath, dinner, reading in bed and lights off at 9 p.m., then chances of her following it every day without much protest are higher. However, if there is no clear routine and the homework can be done anytime she chooses or dinner time changes everyday, then she might push things around as she deems fit and everything might turn into a battle ground. It could vary during the holidays when you make it more flexible with timings that can be stretched a little like 'get ready and finish breakfast by 10 a.m.' or 'finish homework before going to the park in the evening'. Teenagers can be given a choice in making their own time schedule with some basic expectations outlined by you.

A lot of research is being done in the area of habits and one equivocal agreement is that if you want to bring about any change in your life, start with a mini habit, do it daily and it will stay with you for a lifetime. For example, if you want to exercise, rather than promising yourself 90 minutes of workout four times a week in the gym, start with just 10 minutes a day of exercise and slowly build it up. We shall read more about this in the chapter 'Care'. I would also like to point out that it is most important that as parents we also need to follow a routine before we start advocating it to our children. Do remember that children have very sensitive hypocrisy radars.

Recognitions

Recognitions are a very powerful tool in parenting. As I explained in the previous chapter, recognitions are about acknowledging and celebrating the child in front of you. It is about building in the child a sense of worthiness that is authentic and genuine. It is not about praising and making them feel good about themselves but about recognizing and valuing every trait and skill that you want to nurture in them. The former makes them feel they have to please, perform and be perfect in order to get appreciation, whereas the latter builds a solid sense of 'I am valued for who I am right now'. So let's see how recognitions can be used as a coaching tool too. Take an example of a child who is being trained to be more organized. On a scale of 0 to 10, she is on 3 and needs to reach 6:

a. Through **active recognitions** you could highlight the child every time you see her put her things in the proper place: 'I see you have put the books in your school bag.'

b. By giving **value recognitions** you could focus on the skills you want to help build in your child: 'I saw you put the toothbrush and toothpaste back in the mug. I see that your organizational muscles are becoming stronger.'

c. **Proactive recognitions** could be used to highlight the exceptions: 'I did notice that rather than throwing the towel on the floor, you hung it back on the peg. I think the towel looks really happy!'

d. Finally, **creative recognitions** to showcase little opportunities for success. So, after baking a cake, both of you could clear up the kitchen together and you could tell others how your little one 'was so helpful in cleaning up and putting everything back where it belonged'.

Therefore, through recognitions, the child is able to see and build another side to her identity, which is just not 'messy', 'disorganized', 'chaotic' but also 'organized' and 'careful with her things'. We have to water the wholesome seeds rather than just the negativity seeds of lack, deficit and what's wrong.

Externalization

However, you might want to address the 'problem' sometimes, but how can you do that without the child feeling attacked. In Narrative Therapy, we use an approach pioneered by the late Michael White called Externalization. Through this approach, we place the problem outside the child rather than within him and give it a name. So, for example, if the child is struggling with anger we might call the problem Anger and talk to the child as if the Anger was separate from him.

So the questions/statements might go as, 'Did you see how Anger was controlling you yesterday?' (It is best to do this when the child is calm and more receptive.)

'I think Anger is really troubling you nowadays in the evening.'

'Can you make out when Anger is coming close?'

'How do you feel it in your body?'

'Do you see how the Hot Angry Thoughts come along with Anger?'

'What do you think we can do to get rid of this Anger?'

'Can I tell you some tricks that work or me when Anger comes near me?'

It might seem a little bizarre but children take to this slight change in language and approach very well. Personifying feelings, difficulties, imaginations and fantasies come very easily to them. Do remember you have to be consistent in this approach otherwise you might end up confusing the child. If you feel unsure about it or after trying it you feel it does not work, just drop it. It needs practice and a way of thinking (the problem is the problem, the child is not the problem) that does not come easily to most of us. The best part of externalization is that it can be tried with so many issues – anger, tantrums, crankiness, bed-wetting, soiling, laziness, procrastination, etc. I remember when my daughter was little she was going through a phase when she would become a little whiny at times when she was tired or hungry. We would playfully call that mood 'Chimpu' and there was much talk about how 'Chimpu' was troubling Anya and what we needed to do to make it run away and leave Anya alone. This was a sure way to get her giggling and in her usual bubbly, happy mood soon. In fact, very soon she became an expert at detecting 'Chimpu' and would say, 'I think Chimpu is coming, let's throw it quickly before it spoils our fun!'

Boundaries and rules

You might say that parenting is not all about fun and games and could be full of challenges that require tough handling.

These could range from doing homework, establishing bedtimes, insisting on healthy meals, restricting screen time to taking a stand on abusive language, use of alcohol or drugs or maintaining non-violence at home. Boundaries and rules are essential aspects to parenting. Children thrive in homes where there are clear, non-threatening boundaries and rules. Some important points to keep in mind as far as boundaries and rules are concerned:

1. **I like to take a 'Traffic Light Approach' for rules and boundaries:** A red light is for behaviours that need a zero-tolerance, non-negotiable approach. This could range from rules on violence, abusive language, bullying to stipulated screen time. The yellow light could be for behaviours or good habits the child is still learning to master, like sitting down for homework, packing her bag at night, etc. These are skills that the child needs training in with your support. The green light is for behaviours that are all right with you or the ones that you do not want to address right now. For example, you might not want to make an issue of the fact that your child is still coming to your bed in the middle of the night once or twice a week. This approach gives us clarity, lets us choose our priorities and helps us choose our battles. We are not aiming for perfect children but we are working towards helping them grow into independent, responsible and happy human beings.

   Everybody also needs to understand that this rule is just not for children but for everybody at home, including parents, grandparents and domestic help. Children respect rules if they know that there are no double standards about them.

2. **Clear rules work when they are not too many of them:** I would suggest that at a time there should not be more than three rules that children are learning to follow. Too many rules will only confuse them and make them feel resentful. Rules can only be designed keeping the child's ZPD in mind. If you are concerned about your child being physically unfit and overweight then it might be better to start with the fifteen-minute rule of running in the park (if that is the exercise he prefers) in the evening rather than insisting that he has to exercise for one hour a day.

3. **Convince yourself first:** It is important that you convince yourself before you insist he follow that rule. If you think it is all right for your child to hit the domestic help when he is angry then your 'don't hit her, it is a wrong thing to do' will be water off a duck's back. You need to be convinced yourself and your 'No' needs to be conveyed with 100 per cent conviction. Children have very sensitive radars to check if you really mean business or you can be overlooked. Conviction also means that you do not feel guilty about establishing these rules and that you do not take the child's protests personally. You have to be convinced that it is your responsibility to establish these rules. Children will push and protest and try to break non-negotiable/red-light rules—that is part of their wiring but that should not make you doubt your conviction.

4. **Empathize with their discomfort, anger and annoyance at these boundaries:** They will protest, 'Everybody in my class has a phone,' or 'My friend can watch as much TV as he wants in his house.' Listen to them, empathize with, 'I can understand that you must be upset that you get less TV than your friends.' I find it best not to get into long arguments or discussions around these rules. I have found that children do listen and respond positively if you tell them, 'I know you are upset but this is something I have to do as your mother as it is my responsibility.' It sends the message across that you love them enough to lay down tough rules.

5. **Consistency is extremely important:** I would say you have to be consistent in your approach otherwise it makes no sense to establish rules. So, if you have established a rule of 'No hitting' then you cannot cite an excuse for your child hitting out sometimes, saying 'he is just too tired and sleepy right now'. If you have made a red-light rule make sure it is reinforced every time it is broken. There is no point taking up a stand when you are not going to be there to see it through to the end. Can you imagine how chaotic and crazy a football match would become if the referee decided to give the yellow and red card at his whim and fancy? I once heard a very renowned and wise psychotherapist, Dr Salman Akhtar, use the Tarzan metaphor for parenting. He said that children are like Tarzans who have to swing from vine to vine, branch to branch, and that's what makes them who they are. Parents are like the tree they are swinging on. They

have to let them do the swinging but they have to stay grounded and firm, and not let the swinging uproot them!

6. **I do think the crucial ingredient of enforcing boundaries is when parents are united in their approach:** If the mother has made it very clear to the children that they cannot get any screen during weekdays but the father brushes it off as the mother being 'too harsh' then there are chances of the children making use of that divided stand (they are experts on this) and wriggle their way through the cracks to get what they want. For those living in joint families and having live-in domestic help, it becomes even more vital to get everybody on board. It can be really tough as we have very strong feelings about boundaries – for some it can rake up a lot of residual feelings of guilt, maybe pain or fears from their own childhood.

    So, for every boundary you impose, examine your own feelings and try to resolve them before reaching a clear understanding with your partner.

7. **Make that extra deposit in your child's emotional bank account:** Personally, I do find that when I have to enforce a boundary, I make sure I have 'made extra deposits in my children's emotional bank account' so that when the rule is spelt out, it is easier for them to take it in their stride. If I was to do it when my interaction with them is a little strained, then chances of them fighting it tooth and nail are stronger.

8. **Everyone should understand the rules clearly:** It is important that all the family members and domestic help

understand the rules clearly. Some families might reach
the rules after an open discussion with the children, 'We
are all getting late every morning for our school bus and
work. So maybe we need to sit down and have a clear
idea on what time all of us need to get up every morning.
Any ideas?'

Rules established like this are obviously most successful
as everybody carries a sense of ownership and nobody
feels blamed. However, there might be times that the
parents need to outline a rule when the children are not
willing to buy into the discussion. 'I know you do not
agree with us but after some discussion, your father and
I have decided that we need to cut down on TV time.
So the rule from now on is no TV on weekdays. We
understand that this will make you feel upset but our
decision is final.'

9. **Avoid needless discussions**: Once a rule is made 'do
not get into negotiations, discussions or arguments as it
will frustrate everybody' and won't really help. Do not
apologize for your rule, do not repeatedly thank them for
following it and, most of all, do not put it out as questions.
Guess what would be the answer to, 'Hey, kids! Is it all
right if we keep the TV off during the weekdays?' For
some clear rules it is good to have a 'No' at the beginning
so that there is complete clarity.

10. **Do not give repeated warnings**: It is 'best to avoid
repeated warnings' as it gives the children the message
that you really do not mean business. So, if the Wi-Fi has
to be switched off at 10 p.m. do not keep repeating, 'I will

be switching it off soon.' At ten minutes to 10, you warn them to save what they need to and then at 10 o'clock you go right ahead and switch it off.

11. **Reset**: One very important strategy, which I also explained in the previous chapter, I have learned (though I have modified it a little) from the Nurtured Heart Approach by Howard Glasser, is Reset. Reset is about becoming mindful that you are getting into a negativity loop with your child and stepping back. It is about resetting ourselves to higher, better, more effective levels. So when I catch myself in what I like to call the 'cranky mum' state, I quickly move back, take a deep breath, notch up my playfulness quotient a little and come back. This reset could last from a few moments to even half an hour. The quicker it is the better so that you are back in the arena as soon as possible.

12. **Avoid words like 'rules' and 'routines'**: Some children are allergic to the use of words like rules and routines. Let's admit that these are very emotionally loaded words. I met a lovely family recently and the parents told me that they did not have any rules as they did not need them. 'The Connect they had created at home was strong enough to help them function' seamlessly without rules. If you were to start working in a new place, which communication would you prefer? 'There is a rule that everybody has to report by 9 a.m.', or 'Our practice is to be at work by 9 a.m.' So, depending on your children and what you would prefer, I would say that we interchange rules with words like 'procedures',

'This is the way we do things in our home,' 'practices' or even 'boundaries'.

If you are still not very clear about rules and boundaries, I would like you to think of football. I love football and like to use it as a metaphor for life. There have to be clear rules and boundaries while playing a good football game. Imagine how difficult it would be to play football and decide fouls if there were no clearly defined boundary lines. All the players and referees are aware of these rules and there is consistency in maintaining them. Depending on the foul, the referee shows a yellow or red card. The players protest, shout, scream and literally throw tantrums on the field but the referees do not take the protests of the football players personally. They do their job of blowing the whistle, showing the red card and follow it through. They do not get into arguments, discussions or cajoling like, 'I am sorry for this, but please do this for me', 'I am sick and tired of you not listening to me.'

Consequences: What do we do when the non-negotiable/red-light rules are broken?

You might be wondering why I have not used the word discipline yet. The reason is simple; I am a little tired of the word. We talk so much about discipline without really understanding it much.

'We need to teach discipline to our children.'

'Children need to learn self-discipline.'

What is this discipline we keep talking about? We think discipline is about children becoming more acquiescent, obedient and conforming. According to popular notion, discipline is synonymous with parents becoming dictatorial, domineering and overbearing. Discipline is much more than that. It is about children learning to make the right choices and building muscles of self-regulation and responsibility. Discipline is about learning to accept the consequences for the choices they make. Discipline is about building character and not compliance.

As I mentioned earlier, the non-negotiable/red-light rules need to be minimal and primarily about safety and non-negotiable issues like violence, abuse or damaging behaviours. Other issues like studies, bedtime, hygiene, etc., can be handled very well if there is a deep Connect and if the parents follow basic Coaching steps outlined earlier. However, at times, parents need to step in and consider the consequences when the child has broken a non-negotiable/red-light rule. *In fact, children are designed to break rules and that is absolutely fine.* They learn that like everything else in this world, there is a cause and effect to what they do too. So, let's see how it can be implemented.

1. Clearly defined non-negotiable/red-light rules, which could range from no hitting, no abusive language, no screen time during weekdays to no alcohol need to be understood by everybody in the house depending on their age. There also needs to be an acceptance that every time the child breaks the non-negotiable/red-light rule he

will have to bear the consequences. Make sure you have established a procedure in advance that everybody is aware of. It is always helpful if they are given a choice on what consequence they would opt for in case a rule is broken. For a younger child who has hit his baby sister, it could range from making a 'Sorry' card to doing various household chores like watering the plants, cleaning up some shelves in a cupboard, scrubbing the bathtub, weeding a patch in the garden, etc. *The consequence does not have to be unpleasant or harsh, it needs to be any work that makes them put in an effort and assist in the running of the house.* Chances are high that if you have a deep, solid connect with the child and you spell out the procedure without getting all charged up and angry about it, the child will 'pay the dues' and carry on with life. The message is basically, 'Little one, you messed up. What are you doing to pay up?'

2. So stay calm, take it as a learning exercise and do not hold any grudges against the child or keep talking about it once the child has paid up. In fact, I would suggest that you keep speaking very respectfully and calmly to the child. The message to the child should be, 'I love you but I do not agree with your behaviour.'

3. The consequence does not have to be immediate. If the child has watched TV on a non-screen day while you were at work, then you could have the consequence of deducting the screen time during the weekend. I prefer natural consequences, as they are very powerful in helping the child understand that they are responsible for their own behaviour. So, just like adults have to pay

a fine for speeding, get into trouble with their boss if they are late and lose their house if they do not pay their mortgage, children understand that their behaviour also has a consequence. It is a life skill and the early we start it the better.

4. Avoid threats as children do not take them seriously and you lose credibility in their eyes as somebody who is just words and no action and does not need to be taken seriously. So give up your ranting, 'I am going to ground you for a week,' 'I am going to lock your PSP,' and what is most common in India in case little children are being naughty, 'I will call the doctor and he will give you a big injection!'

5. Do not get into power struggles, arguments, and negotiations over non-negotiable/red-light rules. Just state the consequence, clear and simple, and get out of the way. I am totally against punishments as there is no learning in it, the child only feels inadequate, resentful and the parent ends up feeling guilty, confused and disempowered. Watch out for consequences that are actually punishments in disguise. Punishments are reactive, illogical, arbitrary and generally come from a position of anger, 'How dare you? I will teach you a lesson.'

   Whereas natural consequences come from a position of respect and with the goal of building responsibility and making them take ownership of their choices.

6. If you have a strong Connect, you have defined realistic boundaries and there are clear choices children have on

how they would pay up every time they mess up, then the learning is happening. However, if you feel that your child is not responding to this too then you might have to take a decision of taking control. So, for example, a child who is refusing to make a 'Sorry' card for his sister as an apology for hitting her, could be told, 'I can see that you are finding it difficult to take a more responsible choice right now. So I will wait for you to do the apology and only then we will go to the park to play.' The crucial thing here is that as he did not make the responsible choice you have taken charge of what you can control in the situation, i.e., going to the park. This strategy works very well as you do not feel so helpless and 'I can't do anything about it'. If he decides to make the card, then you appreciate his choice and head to the park without any grudges. And if he does not, then you go through the rest of the day without any anger and bitterness as he has already paid for the irresponsible choice by missing the park.

7. As I discussed earlier, *it is important at times to ask rather than just tell*. For example, if your son has got a note in his diary for using an abusive word in the classroom, you could sit with him and reflect on the issue through some questions rather than getting upset with him and blaming him:

'How do you feel about this note?'

'What do you think you need to do to make sure this does not happen again?'

'What consequence do you think you need to bear for breaking this rule?'

8. Do always remember to recognize the responsible choice the child takes for breaking a rule, 'I appreciate that you have taken the right choice and are willing to miss one hour of TV on Saturday for breaking the rule that we had decided to follow.'

Therefore, through the steps I have outlined earlier, the children are learning that you have some basic expectations as far as their behaviour is concerned. They are also learning that you accept the breaking of rules as long as they are able to follow the consequences. In the end, what they are learning is that they always have a choice and that the choice impacts their quality of life, their relationships and how their life would unfold.

Can Talent be Bred?

Another essential element of coaching is honing talent in our children. It's really interesting to see the way we see talent as an all or none phenomenon. Either you have it or you don't. Typically we hear, 'she's so talented' or 'he has no talents at all'. They are seen as precious gems waiting to be discovered at the right time and then the child can live happily ever after once he has reaped the benefits of this talent.

Then how do you explain the child prodigies who show their brilliance in dance, music, chess and sports and fade away after outshining the others once? What happens to their talent?

Our brain has around trillion neurons which function

through some established circuits. Let's say two children start to learn how to play the piano. When they start on a scale of 0 to 10, Child A, due to his inborn flair for music is on 6 and Child B on 3. Child A wows everybody with his gift and there is much talk about him being a child prodigy. However, he does not practise and tinkers with the piano once in a while when he feels like it. Therefore, his skill level does not improve or maybe deteriorates with time.

On the other hand, Child B is in love with the piano and passionately practises everyday. What is happening to his brain wiring? The music circuit of the brain is getting stronger and stronger, developing myelin sheathing (somewhat like insulated casing that allows the circuit to work more speedily, accurately and efficiently), which helps him to move from 3 to 8 on the same scale. Imagine it like a small lane, which, with repeated use and allocation of resources, turns into a super-efficient expressway! As Daniel Coyle explains in his book, *The Talent Code*, 'Skill circuits that are fired more will receive more broadband (myelin).'

So what about amazing talents like Sachin Tendulkar, Mozart or Van Gogh? They obviously had the inborn gift but it became a genuine talent only when it was combined with dedicated practice and passion. What do Beatles, Mozart and Bill Gates have in common? Malcolm Gladwell in his landmark book, *Outliers*, highlighted research that showed that it takes more that 10,000 hours of practice to become an outlier. Despite all the child prodigy talk, Mozart is believed to have produced his most brilliant compositions after twenty years of composing music.

I have a simple formula for nurturing talent. Natural flair + deep practice + passion + nurturing environment = Greatness.

Tips for Talent Whisperers

1. **Asset and affinity:** Asset is what the child has and affinity is what the child is inclined towards. Magic can only happen if there is an overlap between the two. There is no point pushing a child who is good at dancing to dance when she has no interest in shaking a leg. So let them explore and experiment with various things before they find something they truly love.

2. **Connect, play and master:** This is the sequence best trainers take to build mastery. A child will only open up if he/she feels valued and in turn values his/her relationship with the coach. They need to be allowed to play, have fun with what they love before they actually attain mastery.

3. **Flow and deep practice:** It is fascinating to see a child who is in the flow (as described by psychologist Mihaly Csikszentmihalyi) dancing, perfecting a football move, strumming a guitar or playing chess. They have no sense of time and are completely immersed in what they love to do. Behind those seemingly uneventful repetitions, the brain is producing myelin, the unsung hero, which helps them master their skill.

4. **Let go of the driving seat:** Most of all, remember, it is about them and not about us. If the child has the rage to master then no force can really stop him/her. However, if there is

no rage, your pushing will not help at all. Instead, it will just snuff out any little spark that might have been present.

Temper Tantrums

A lot of parents struggle with their children's temper tantrums so I am going to briefly address this. I think temper tantrums in toddlers is generally of two types.

Emotional meltdowns

You have to experience one to know what I am talking about here. The child might be fine one moment and suddenly, due to any provocation, he starts to cry and wail. There is deep anguish in the crying and no amount of reasoning at that time will help him regain control. At such a time, if the parents walk away, giving the child some time or try to ignore the unhappy child, the crying escalates into a severe meltdown – red face, floppy body, closed eyes and high-pitched wailing. This kind of tantrum can be understood as a breakdown in the emotional thermostat of the child where the frontal lobe in charge of the clear, rational thinking shuts down and the emotional brain (the limbic system) takes over, causing an emotional hijack.

How to handle emotional meltdowns?

Just hold the child gently on your lap, facing front, and start rubbing his back with soft soothing sounds. Make sure you keep your face away from the head banging otherwise you might end up with a black eye. The child needs to know that you are around and it is almost as if you were taking over as the child's 'surrogate frontal lobe' till he calms down. The important thing to add here is that just because a child is having a meltdown does not mean he ends up getting what was refused to him earlier. You can gently empathize with how he is feeling but retain your stand the whole time. For example, you could say, 'I know you felt really upset when the TV was switched off. It must be so unpleasant to stop watching something you were clearly enjoying so much.' After the child sobs and agrees to that you carry on with, 'But you do remember, sweetheart, that 8 o'clock is bedtime. Let's see which one of your favourite stories we can read today.' With that you tickle the child, scoop him up in your arms and take him to the bedroom. Battle averted, both mum and child end up feeling good about themselves!

Designed tantrums

This kind of tantrum is typical when a child learns as she grows up and becomes an expert on which parental button to press before she ends up getting what she really wants. So you take the child to the mall and before you know it, there is a demand for a new game. As you rush from one store to another, ticking off shopping from your list, she whines away at you, 'Please, Mamma, please.' At times the demand cranks up to cajoling, coaxing, nagging and blackmailing, 'My friends have all these games as their parents love them so much.' Before you know it, the child is throwing a full-blown tantrum, running away from you, hitting you, shouting out or rolling on the floor. And most hapless, guilty parents, for the sake of peace, give in to the demand thus reinforcing the basic belief, 'If I really persist, I will get my way always'.

How to handle designed tantrums?

Let us take the same example we discussed in the previous section. Be proactive and stick to your word. I would suggest that parents have a clear understanding with the child before they venture out. 'We are going to the mall to shop for shoes. We will not buy any toys. If anybody starts demanding anything that is not on the list, then we will pack up and come back immediately. Deal?' The important thing is that you stick to the deal. It will be inconvenient and frustrating but remember, you are giving a clear message to the child. Also, it is extremely important that you do it with respect and no negative emotions. The parents end up feeling empowered and the child gets an important message – 'I cannot get my way by whining or throwing a tantrum.'

Sense of entitlement

As parents, we despair at our children's growing sense of entitlement. However, we have to ask ourselves about how much we have cultivated it in them too? How many parents really expect their children to pitch in with the household chores like making their own beds, laying the table, helping in the kitchen or doing the dishes? Their sense of entitlement stems from our own overprotectiveness. We want to buffer our children from all sorts of discomfort as much as possible and try to keep them happy all the time. That obviously is not really going to help them grow and acquire a healthy sense of responsibility.

So make sure that you discuss with them from a very young age how the running of the house has to be a joint responsibility and, depending on their age, get them to do their chores. They will moan, groan and complain but do not take it personally. Empathize with their discomfort but let them know, la Spiderman style, 'With greater power comes greater responsibility!'

Emotionally intense children

Some children are emotionally very intense. That is the way they are wired and parenting them can be an uphill task as they can turn out to be high-maintenance. They demand, push boundaries, react noisily, have meltdowns, scream, shout and fight. They are the ones who the teachers complain about the most. They are the ones who drain every ounce of their parents' energy. They are the ones who, if not handled very well at an early age, can turn out to be the ones who get into drugs, alcohol and other high-risk behaviours. It is as if their emotional/limbic system brain has hijacked their thinking/frontal brain.

These children need this approach notched up to another level. They need a higher level of Connect with regular daily doses of Recognitions as if the parents' life depended on it. They need a much more involved, 'in the trenches', hands-on Coaching. Parenting has to be done courageously and compassionately and needs to become a daily practice with these parents.

Reflection

GPS Checklist

I would suggest that whenever you do feel that things are going a little off track and you are not sure what to do, go through the checklist of ten questions given below. It is like a Global Positioning System (GPS) check for all of us parents to stop, pause and reflect on what could possibly be going wrong in their Coaching approach:

1. Do I have a deep, rich connect with my child?
2. What is the level of my emotional deposits right now?
3. Am I giving enough recognition to the child?
4. What seeds am I watering?
5. Are my expectations realistic? Are they in keeping with my child's ZPD?
6. Is my CP hooking the RC of the child?
7. What do I need to do to connect to her Adult?
8. Am I giving my relationship with my child adequate 'hands-on' focus?
9. Are the boundaries clear and consistent?
10. Am I convinced about the non-negotiable/red-light rules and can implement the consequences without any negativity?

I have made these questions a daily practice for myself to check my relationship with my children.

It is not enough to say that I love my children and that will take care of everything. Love is no spectator sport. Love is a daily practice of rolling up the sleeves and jumping into the arena, sweating it out, putting in every bit of our heart and soul and then stepping back at the end of the day, exhausted but full of exultation – I did my best! There will be days when you will feel that you slipped up big time, but that's all right. Soul work is a journey and there will be bumps and falls. Just get up, be compassionate to yourself, dust off the dirt and move on.

3

CONNECT
AND COACH FOR
TEENAGERS

$\mathcal{N}$ow, when our own kids have grown older (sixteen and twelve), my husband and I love to sit back and reflect on the different stages of their life. Nothing gives us more joy and pleasure (and teary eyes) than looking at their old photographs and videos. It is like their lives are etched like live photo albums in our mind – full of colour, light and energy. Obviously, we have had our share of pain, fears and frustration but they have been fine too.

In this chapter, I would like to just pause and look at this stage of tween and teen from the age of twelve to eighteen, taking them from middle to senior school. I think that in the present day and age, the middle school is one of the most challenging phases. Suddenly our little babies, who were happy in the world of Harry Potter, Disney movies and giggly sleepovers, are suddenly turning into these uber cool tweens with crushes, becoming aware of their changing bodies, trying to develop their own style or blindly copying others. They start connecting through Instagram, Facebook, Snapchat and what have you. On one hand, their friendships become deeper, they can do so much more and the world seems much more exciting and liberating than it was when they were in junior school. However, social hierarchies are formed, which tend to continue till the end of high school. Images and reputations are created and at times even if they try, it is difficult for them to shrug them off. Everybody has already decided what they are like and how they are going to be.

As they grow older and move to high school, a lot of things start changing for them. If things go well for them (and that is saying a lot), then high school can be a great time for kids. They get more sense of freedom, the scope of fun widens even further and the world is full of possibilities. However, let us admit it, school is a bit like a battleground for most teenagers. For a lot of high-schoolers, going to school is like getting ready for war every day. Submissions, projects, board exams, social hierarchies, bullying, preoccupation, near obsessiveness with their own bodies, competiveness, finding a boyfriend or girlfriend (you are obviously a looser if you don't have one), split-ups, rumours that go viral and what not. Teachers that crank up the pressure (and stop smiling), parents who stop listening (and start harassing). It is a far cry from the nurturing, caring space that the child stepped in, maybe, ten years ago.

Parenting a teenager is quite different from parenting a child. This is the time you are stepping back and letting them slowly take charge of their lives. 'It's my life' is a phrase that parents get to hear more often. However, there is still some confusion as we see that despite their hulk-like bodies and attitude of 'I can manage very well without you', they still struggle in day to day things. There are some who seem to thrive and manage the growing demands with ease but there are many of the 'late bloomers' variety who seem to be just spiralling down. To fathom adolescence better, it's very important to understand the brain behind it.

Teenage Brain – Work in Progress

Visualize trying to navigate your way in a city. At every

turn there is some construction work, which impedes your progress. Most of the familiar routes have been blocked and there is no proper signposting. The wide network of roads, junctions, crossroads, highways and flyovers are not being managed efficiently, causing traffic jams, accidents and a general grid lock. How would you feel? Confused, irritable, defiant and grumpy?

If roads were the neurons and the interconnections the synapses (a structure that permits a neuron to pass a chemical or an electric signal to another neuron), then the chaotic city is not very different from an adolescent's brain. Neuroscientists are challenging conventional wisdom, which narrowed down teenage behaviour to raging hormones. New research indicates that the brain undergoes some fundamental restructuring during adolescence. It starts 'pruning' or clearing away half the neural connections that we make in early childhood. According to Sharon Bagley, neuroscientist and author of *Train Your Mind and Change Your Brain*, some 20 billion synapses are pruned every day from childhood to adolescence. They disappear like baby fat. It definitely has come as a shock as it was believed that the brain was fully formed by puberty. The same brain that might have functioned quite seamlessly till the age of eleven or twelve suddenly becomes a chaotic 'work in progress'.

The neural pathways that are maintained are those that carry heavy traffic; those that dissolve are like unused bylanes, railway lines, going out of business. Pruning follows a simple principle of 'Use it or Lose it'. There is significant pruning of the frontal lobe, which is responsible for clear thinking, executive functions, high-level reasoning and decision-making. That explains a lot of impulsive, irrational thinking at this age. Research indicates that the girls start their pruning about a year before the boys but the end result is the same.

Before you hit the panic button, I must clarify that this stage is an essential part of neurodevelopment. Unproductive or weak connections are pruned in much the same way a gardener would prune a tree or a bush, giving the plant a healthier structure. This phase of rewiring might lead to a lot of typical turbulent adolescent behaviour but it is required before the brain shapes up into a sophisticated, efficient hub of rich yet streamlined processing paths. It is only when the person is twenty or twenty-one that the brain matures into the finely tuned neural circuitry.

To top it, the hormonal changes during this phase create further ripples. What is most interesting is that the female teen brain is very different from that of the male at that age. In girls, the estrogen surges in puberty suddenly make them more prone to be self-consciousness, emotionally susceptible and with a higher need for connection. Oxytocin, another hormone that takes on a major role in developing their maternal instinct and nurturance later, also starts kicking in big time. Teenaged girls get a surge of this happy hormone when they are connecting, talking and bonding with their peer group.

On the other hand, the male teen brain is slightly different. After puberty, boys have ten times more testosterone pumping through their systems and it affects their need for speed, participation in competitive sports, building of muscles and they get territorial. Not only that, they also start seeking the testosterone rush by pushing themselves and indulge in risk-taking behaviours. You might get exasperated with your son's tendency to get into repeated trouble and ask, 'Why weren't you thinking?' Maybe he was too busy tripping on the testosterone to really think about the consequences!

What is also very interesting is that when they hit a rough patch, boys tend to externalize (get aggressive, break boundaries, take risks, resort to rage), whereas girls tend to internalize (withdraw, get anxious, become depressed and develop eating disorders).

Simple mantras that the brain follows at this stage are 'Use it or Lose it' and 'Neurons that fire together wire together'. The first mantra basically means that as the brain prunes itself, those parts of it which are being used and exercised stay and the ones that are not are snipped off. If two kids learned to play the guitar and only one continued to practise it in the teens while the other stopped, chances of the first one turning out to be a skilled musician are higher in his adult life than the latter, even if the second kid tried picking it up later in life.

The second mantra, 'Neurons that fire together wire together' can be explained through the same city roads metaphor. Our brain operates through different kinds of networks, much like the road network. In a city, places with roads that are used more frequently become better connected, they are made wider, smoothened out and better maintained. Similarly, in the brain, the parts that are used together get stronger connections. A teenager who gets up early in the morning to go for a jog (a rare phenomenon for a teenager though) has higher chances of associating mornings with physical activity. Similarly, another teenager who gets into the habit of eating junk food while watching TV might associate TV with mindless munching.

Understanding teens is not easy; the field is vast and possibly material for another book. Nevertheless, I highlighted these neuro-structural and neurochemical changes to lay emphasis on some of the 'storms and stresses' of this phase and how understanding it is crucial for every parent. There is another way of looking at this. The teenage brain is constructed to experiment, explore and be adventurous. It is more open to ideas, rebels against status quo and craves for change. And that is what is exciting about this age till our brain gets too set in its ways.

Teenage Lifestyle

Sleep: If I was asked one recent trend in children that I find alarming, I would definitely say their sleep pattern. After a day in school, which runs into tuitions, activity classes, homework, a late dinner with parents who return late from work, it is about 10 p.m. that a child gets time to unwind. And what does she do? Park herself in front of the TV or computer to unwind, play and indulge in social networking before hitting the bed. Many teenagers I meet nowadays admit that they do not get to sleep till 2 or 3 a.m. in the morning. Then they are up again at 6 a.m. or so, rushing to catch the bus and somehow plough through the day, catching a few winks during the 'boring periods' to start the whirlwind of their afterschool treadmill again.

Let's look at some hard-hitting research in the area of sleep:

- Contrary to popular myth, a teenage brain requires at least eight hours of sleep every night. It is during sleep that the brain of a teenager develops and consolidates. Chronic sleep deprivation can cause permanent damage to his/her brain's neuro-structuring. There are also implications of how this can disrupt the human growth hormone.

- Sleep loss can deactivate our body's ability to extract glucose from the blood stream. In children it can lead to problems like inattention, impulsivity, difficulty in learning and memorizing (as it is during sleep that we crystallize our memory).

- Lack of adequate sleep increases the hormone ghrelin, which increases hunger, and suppresses its metabolic opposite leptin, which suppresses appetite. Therefore, research indicates that inadequate sleep could play a big role in why our children are becoming more obese.

- Sleep loss also elevates the stress hormone – cortisol. This is turn can make our children more moody, irritable and even depressed and anxious if the pattern becomes chronic.

- Getting them back on track can be challenging. This is especially true for teenagers whose melatonin levels (the neuro-chemical that indicates that it is dark and time to sleep) kicks in later by ninety minutes than for children and adults. And the constant flicker of TV and computer screens does not really help their biological clock to function well. There are some schools in the US, which are bringing in later school hours for teenagers to accommodate changing biorhythms.

Electronic and social media: We are all victims of these now – smart phones, gaming consoles, ipods, laptops, computers, TVs. We cannot get enough of them and we cannot live without them. Our lives are ruled by them. However, for a teenager, this attraction can turn to severe addiction. In our clinics we see teenagers regularly who are seriously addicted to them. When I say addicted I do not mean it in a loose sense. I mean serious addiction – where these young people reach a point where they have stopped going to school, socializing and leading a regular life. I am sure it is important to point out here that there is always a deeper emotional problem that pushes a younger person to prefer the virtual world to the real one. But again, going back to the brain, what is really happening there? Research indicates that the reward centres in our brain (think chocolate) usually associated with addiction can get really charged up whenever children and teenagers are gaming or interacting on social media. Every level achieved or 'like' is a testosterone high for boys and every 'like' on the social media is an oxytocin trip for girls. A typical example of 'Neurons that fire together wire together.' They learn to seek their daily dose of highs through electronic and social media.

Ravish's story

Ravish's parents were extremely worried about their sixteen-year-old son. He spent all his time in front of his laptop, playing games on the internet and watching Youtube videos. Any attempt on the parents' part to get him to lead a regular life was met with angry outbursts and breaking of things. In their desperation, they tried switching off the Wi-Fi and hiding his laptop but that led to extreme aggression, threats of running away from home or committing suicide.

We meet many children like Ravish in our centre who struggle with intense forms of internet addiction. Most of the times, after careful interaction with the child and family we get to understand that there is always an underlying problem that triggers off this addiction. It could range from depression, anxiety, social difficulties, family conflict, etc., which the child is trying to escape from. As Ravish shared with me, 'I hate myself, I hate my life. The only time I feel good is when I am playing with my (virtual) friends on the laptop.'

Even as adults we often find ourselves straddling the real and virtual worlds at the same time. Youtubing, Tweeting, Facebooking, streaming, downloading, Instagramming, blogging, vlogging and messaging are happening at the same time as we work, interact, drive and parent. We are all addicts and addicted to something in the spectrum.

Baroness Susan Greenfield, neuroscientist at Oxford University, in her book, *Mind Change*, draws upon the analogy of climate change to bring our attention to how the digital world is changing the wiring of our brains.

A joke that Anya, my daughter, cracks all the time:

Question: How can you find your children in the house?

Answer – By switching off the Wi-Fi!

We live in a world where we judge our sense of worth from the number of 'likes', 'friends' and 'followers' we have. At work, we cannot resist sneaking a quick peek to see if the latest tweet has got any re-tweets. At dinner time in your favourite restaurant with our family, rather than relishing the togetherness we are more preoccupied about getting the right shot of the Lobster Thermidor so that we can post it on Instagram to show everybody what a good time we are having! So, you can just imagine, with all that we know about them now, how gullible teenagers can be to this. Psychologist Howard Gardner, very aptly calls them the 'app generation'!

On a holiday to Italy, I was struck by how a couple of teenagers were quibbling with each other about who had got more immediate likes on his Facebook photo of the colosseum. I guess the thrills of the 'likes' totally outweighed the awe-inspiring grandeur around them. I am sure you would agree that holidays have become more about showing off on social media than actually being there.

Another thing that troubles me about social media is the artificial profiles with all those cleverly self-promotional, photoshopped pictures and updates. I have seen 'selfies' of young tweens in various contorted suggestive positions and adults raving about how 'hot' she looked. Am I the only one who is shocked! I could never imagine them saying anything like that in real life. It is as if we are leading two separate lives with two different personalities – virtual and real. Recently, I was even more dismayed when one of the leading cosmetic companies launched a range of face creams that are supposed to miraculously give you stunningly beautiful 'selfies'. Talk about exploiting the vulnerabilities of the teens to the hilt!

I know you might tell me about the research, which has indicated that social media makes people feel more connected and that it can help promote awareness of important issues and causes. I get that, but I see too many problems with it for me to think otherwise. Talk to any teenager and he/she would tell you that one of their biggest nightmare is to have a rumour spread about them on social media. The bullying or the 'snarking' that happens in tween and teen circles is startling. However, no matter how much it might trouble some of us, social media is here to stay. So, rather than raving and ranting about it (which is exactly what I end up doing sometimes), we need to have more conversations about it with our kids and see how we can make them more media savvy and responsible.

Diet and sedentary lifestyle: A friend jokingly commented that her kids were Italian as they only liked pasta and pizza. Our children's diets are nothing like ours when we were their age. Most urban kitchens run as per the dictates of these fussy age group, and when disappointed with what is kept in front of them, they are quick to order in food. High intake of junk food, sugar, caffeine, fizzy drinks and very low intake of vegetables, fruits and wholesome meals is the trend. Couple it with a sedentary lifestyle, hunching in front of laptops for hours and we have alarming statistics for obesity, mood swings, early orthopaedic problems and what not!

Social context: If I were to describe in one word what most parents of teenagers experience, it would be confusion. On one hand, we have more information on parenting than was ever possible. Go to the Amazon site and just type in parenting in their search engine and you get close to a million results. I am not even talking about the number of blogs, websites or magazines that have sprouted in the past few decades. We are living in the world of hyper parenting. However, are we any more wise or confident than our parents? I don't think so. We might have all the information in the world but we have decreased clarity.

What do we do?

I can totally relate with the feeling of helplessness that a lot of parents are battling with. However, as always, I like to use the inside-out approach to help us out of this quagmire. There are certain things we can't change – the emotional turbulence of teens due to their yo-yoing hormones and 'pruning' brains, the high levels of demands placed by the social context on them and the explosion of electronics and social media.

They might not be able to manage some of their emotions and behaviour but with your understanding of what they are going through, you might need to move away from the victimized parent ('I am so stressed about his irresponsible behaviour') and focus on how you can be a more effective parent. Critical and 'nagging' parenting ('You are just whiling away time' or 'Work hard now, you have the rest of your life to enjoy') will only push them further into chaos. They might not be able to change their behaviour but we can change ours. It is also important to keep in mind that parental anxiety is also high during this age. We are worried about their studies, sleep, diet, friends, safety and so on and so forth. So, adult time for teenagers means questions, lectures and demands. A pressure they would rather do without.

Thus, every bit of what we went through in the previous chapters, Connect and Coach, are applicable to teenagers too. However, I am going to just highlight three aspects of parenting that become extremely essential during this stage.

Listen

We have heard how important it is to communicate with our teenagers. Lot of the problems are attributed to 'lack of communication', 'communication breakdown' or 'strained communication'. We believe that at the core of a good relationship is talking and speaking. That is the reason when our teenagers are going through difficult phases we like to tell them, 'Let's sit and talk' or 'We need to discuss'. What if I told you that all our sitting and talking is actually more damaging than helpful for children, especially adolescents?

Let us choose a typical scenario. You want to talk to your teenaged son about his irresponsible behaviour. What is the first reaction you get when you ask him, 'Can we talk?' He might roll his eyes and let out a heavy sigh that says, 'Here we go again' and brace himself for a long lecture. As you start with your, 'We need to talk', he sits slumped in front of you, eyes glazing over slowly with a look that can be best described as 'whatever'. You try to be as kind as possible, choosing your words with care, peppered with, 'You know we want the best for you', 'It is in your best interest', but soon you get irritated, as he does not seem to be responding at all. You finally lose your cool when you see him looking at his watch furtively and shout out, 'You are not really bothered, are you?' He responds with, 'Not really', and soon the so-called talk transforms into a heated argument and some door slamming. Both parties go away feeling angry, helpless and confused. All this talking is supposed to work, right? Wrong.

Let us look at some basics of communication to get your relationship with your teenager off the 'whatever' stage:

1. **Listening before talking**: The most important part of communication is listening and not talking. And listening deeply 'instead of just waiting for your turn to speak' (*Fight Club*, one of my favourite movies!). One complaint I hear from teenagers about their parents is that 'they do not understand as they never listen'. For many parents, 'Let's talk' is mainly about 'I will talk and you will listen'. It should be the other way around, 'You talk and I will listen'. So take interest in what your child does, spend time together to get to know her world, listen without judging (especially not their friends) and

you will be surprised at what she will be ready to share with you.

2. **Make it casual**: Rather than that big talk which will always get their 'uh-oh' antennae up, make it brief, make it casual, without going, 'I need to talk to you about something'. It could be done while you are dropping him to the bus stop or when you are clearing the table after a meal. Teenagers are particularly allergic to lectures and long speeches so cut out the spiel. With them you have to find these micro slots to engage them. I sometimes go and park myself in my teenage son's room. If he asks me, 'What are you doing here?' I just say casually, 'Nothing, just want to be here.' After some time, as there is no barrage of demands or questions, he tends to start a conversation and before you know it we are having a deep meaningful chat.

3. **Send invitations:** Try sending them invitations like, 'I would love to go out for a coffee with you sometime this week. Let me know when it is convenient. Don't worry, just coffee – no lecture.' Remember, despite all the prickliness and 'I don't care' attitude, they will love you for hanging in there.

4. **Switch channels**: A mother I met recently was very worried about her strained relationship with her daughter. Any attempt on her part to connect was met with a solid firewall. After our discussion, she decided to write a long letter to her daughter. She wrote a most beautiful letter in which she told her daughter how much she loved her and what her daughter meant to her. The mother came back to me after a week with a big smile and

a 'I have got my daughter back'! You could even email, SMS, Instagram or leave little post-its.

Respect

Responsible teens are an oxymoron. But I think that it is more to do with our perception of them and the way we like to pigeonhole them. 'These teenagers have no sense of time.' 'They are so self-centred.' 'Not bothered about their future', etc.

I believe teenagers can be responsible if we respect them and give them a chance to be responsible. We are so busy 'telling' them all the time what to do, what not to do, what is right and what is wrong that it is no surprise that they end up doing just the opposite.

Also, as I had highlighted in the previous chapter, more than how we talk to our children, we need to think about how we talk about them. Make sure you are continuing to spread stories of worthiness, ability and wonder about them. It means a lot to them.

Choice: It is tough letting them make a choice because we feel that they will always end up making the wrong one. I have noticed that whenever I have a strong need to 'tell' my teenaged son what he is doing is wrong, it really does not work. On the other hand, if I step back and let him choose, he mostly ends up making the right choice. It is as if my stepping back gives him the chance to think and look at the consequences of his choices clearly. By choosing they end up with a sense of ownership and take responsibility for their decision.

Reflect: If they do mess up, which they will, try to avoid the 'I told you so' and inevitable berating. Instead, ask them to self-reflect. By asking questions like, 'What do you think happened?' 'Are you all right about getting low scores in your exams?' 'What do you think you would like to do?' help them to self-evaluate, take ownership of their choices, their lives and make them feel empowered.

Pitfalls: Be reflective and not reflexive. The typical ways parents want to build responsibility in their children is through 'telling' (It is high time you started becoming more responsible!), rewards (You get above 90 per cent and I will get you a new mobile!), threats or punishments (We will cut off the internet connection as you are spending too much time on Facebook!). We all do these despite knowing that they do not work. They are born of our own frustration and anxiety and they only make our teens more distant and aloof.

Let them go: They act before thinking, react strongly, explore, experiment and take risks but these are necessary milestones, or rites of passage for them to step into adulthood. When I say let them go, I don't mean let them party all night, not take responsibility or lead a reckless life. I mean that by the time they are thirteen let them go and explore the neighbourhood, manage simple shopping, keep track of their own money; by sixteen let them travel on their own on metros, choose their internships, manage their time, do their own shopping, plan their own parties. At the age of fifteen, I got admission to a college in another city. My parents came to drop me on my first day but after that I managed everything on my own – college, hostel life, shopping, cleaning, washing and bank account. I think that one of the best things they did for me was to have faith in me: 'We know you will be able to manage fine.'

We have to learn to let go gradually. It is most tempting to hold on in the belief that we know better and we don't want our children to make the same mistakes but that is not going to help them at all.

The simple truth is that if you treat teenagers with respect as if they were responsible then they will rise up to the bar you are setting for them. Similarly, if you treat them with disrespect and see them as irresponsible then they will scrape rock bottom to prove to you that they can't be bothered.

Hang In There

Imagine an extremely powerful car with an unskilled driver. That's what your teenager is. So claim the power back, spell out the boundaries and be consistent. There are enough confused parents of teenagers who are walking on egg shells, not sure of where to draw the line. Sit down and discuss the limits with your teenager. It could be about late-night parties, screen time, their pocket money. Follow the 'You, Me, We Approach.' First listen to their point of view, after listening you can put your point across very calmly. Chances are high that if you already have a deep connect and you have listened deeply, he will be ready to reach a solution with you. It is important that you discuss the consequences for the non-negotiable/red-light rules that he will be ready to take if he does not follow through. They might get rude, irritable, shout about how you are treating them like kids, but make sure you stay calm and respectful. They need to understand that you are not imposing these limits because you want to make their life difficult, treat them like kids or show them who the boss is but because these are life skills they need to learn. The message that they are getting is 'I am loved, I am respected but there are clear limits.'

Recently, a sixteen-year-old boy who comes to me for therapy, shared an interesting experience with me. He had arranged to go for a late-night party with a friend. After getting permission from his own parents, he went to his friend's house to pick him up. When he reached there, his friend's parents sat both of them down and started asking them questions like, 'Who all would be there?' 'Will his parents be there?' 'Would there be alcohol or drugs?' 'How late would the party go on?' After some discussion, when they found out that the people who had invited them were known for drug-fest (marijuana, coke, ecstasy, LSD) parties, they told them that they could not give them permission to go. Both of them were upset but the parents did not relent. They told them that they could order a pizza, watch a movie or do anything to have fun at home. The reason this young man shared this experience with me was because it deeply pained him and made him question his own parents. He sat in front of me with tears in his eyes and asked, 'Do my parents not love me enough that they never bothered to ask me these questions?'

So, whatever your teenager might be going through, hang in there. Because behind all that 'can't be bothered' attitude is still a child who is, maybe, as fearful as he was when you dropped him off at the school gate in Nursery. When he rages at you and says he hates you (every teenager feels that even if they do not say so), listen to him. Do not take it personally as he still has years to have a better relationship with you. He might be raging at the world and that is fine too. It is as much a milestone in his life as the tantrum at two or the crush at the age of twelve. He needs to know that you can contain all that fury and that you still love him or her. Do remember, it is a phase too and in between these phases he will come and snuggle up to you and share some bits of his world.

Also, let us not forget that if we have seen one teenager then we have seen one teenager. I might have made some generalizations in this chapter on the basis of research, my experiences as a parent and as a therapist. However, we all know that adolescence is a unique rite of passage for each child. For some it hits early, for some it comes late (some, of course, prefer to remain in this stage for most of their lives), for some it is a smooth transition and for others it is a heart-wrenchingly painful process. Whatever it might be, I know as a parent, it has helped me to dig deeper into myself, to be a less reactive or judgemental parent and become more accepting, containing and reflective.

I have found solace in the serenity so many times, 'Grant

me the serenity to accept the things I cannot change, courage to change the things I can, and the wisdom to know the difference.'

Reflection

1. How deep is your Connect with your teenager?
2. How much are you able to accept your teenager for the person he/she is without trying to change him/her?
3. Are you able to listen to your teenager without getting judgemental?
4. Are you able to define limits with your teenager?

4

CARE

'What we are teaches the child far more than what we say, so we must be what we want our children to become.'

—Joseph Chilton Pearce, American author

*P*arenting can be extremely frustrating, especially when faced with children who are just not getting it right. They might be messy, disorganized, rude, with no sense of time or maybe terrible in math, not coordinated enough to play sports and so on and so forth. It can be extremely tough for parents – constant arguments, shouting matches, daily battles – which can leave everybody drained.

This is not what you had bargained for when you had thought of becoming a parent one day. The feeling of burning out, self-doubt, guilt and a creeping sense of regret. Yes, regret. Not many parents will admit to this forbidden feeling but there is truth in this harsh sentiment. According to a study cited by the famous happiness expert Daniel Gilbert in his book, *Stumbling on Happiness*, the mother's sense of satisfaction decreases after giving birth to a baby and only increases when the children leave home. Parenting children is a lot of hard work but ask any parent what gives them maximum joy and they will point to the little imp running her down with his screams and demands. Paradoxical but so true!

I remember as a new mum, the thing that used to petrify me was the fact that the buck stops with us and that this little human being's life was completely dependent on me and my husband. Sleepless nights, obsessing about every ounce of milk taken in or morsel rejected, trips to the doctor, first step taken, first word heard or imagined, first day at school, they are all etched in our mind forever. And the guilt we carry for everything that does not go well. 'I am a terrible mother as I can't even control my children.' 'I am sure everybody must be thinking I am a bad mother, that's why my child is not doing well in studies.' Shame, guilt, self-blame and embarrassment become our nagging companions. We are so quick to judge ourselves for everything we do or believe we do wrong.

Studies have unequivocally proven one fact – the emotional well-being of the parents, especially the mother, is the key to a child's well-being. So I am only going to focus on your well-being in this chapter. Remember the inflight security announcement? In case of lack of oxygen, first take care of yourself, then your child. Same goes for parenting.

There are endless discussions and so much research on what is good and not good for children: stay-at-home mothers, working mums, single mothers, parents who live together, divorced parents, young mothers, mature mothers, and nuclear and joint families. I have a simple belief – a happy mother is the best thing for children. Children thrive when they have mothers who are happy, joyous and ready to enjoy with them. So, if you have been obsessing about how being a working mother, you have not been able to give the best to your children, then just relax. Children would rather have a mother who is happy when she is with them than a mother who is with them all the time but miserable. Make a choice that builds your sense of growth and well-being. It could be about being a stay-at-home or a working mother, or a single mother. Choose happiness!

Joy and Happiness

> 'One is not always happy when one is good, but one is always good when one is happy.'
>
> —Oscar Wilde, Irish writer and poet

> 'One of the secrets of a happy life is continuous small treats.'
>
> —Iris Murdoch from *The Sea, The Sea*

What makes life worth living are the little joys we experience every day. An early morning cup of tea in the balcony, an invigorating shower, hot toast with butter for breakfast, a heartwarming song on the radio as you drive to work and your favourite bowl of ice cream after dinner. These are not big things but tiny little things that make a lot of difference in our quality of life.

I loved the way Brené Brown described joy as twinkling lights in her book, *The Gifts of Imperfection*.

Twinkling lights are the perfect metaphor for joy. Joy is not a constant. It comes to us in moments – often ordinary ones. Sometimes we miss out on the bursts of joy because we're too busy chasing down extraordinary moments. At other times we are so afraid of the dark that we don't dare let ourselves enjoy the light.

The dark does not destroy the light; it defines it.

I would suggest that you make a 'five-joy diet' – five things that you would do every day to pepper your life with more joy. For that, first make a list of your joys. Write down all the things that bring you pleasure. It could be really bizarre, 'no-big deal' things but write them down anyway. Then make sure every day you include at least five of them. For example, for me, on some day my five joys might be listening to my daughter play her guitar and sing; listening to our favourite music with my husband; doing my Zentangle (more about that later); taking a brisk walk in the park and reading a book in bed before sleeping.

Somehow we believe happiness is out there somewhere in the distant future after we get a hefty paycheck, a perfect body or when our children get to go to a good college. An elusive dream, which is so hard to pin down. However, the simple fact is that it is very much within us. Happiness is a matter of choice. No matter what the circumstances are, we can still choose to be happy. However, there are three points I would like to highlight about happiness first:

• Mihaly Csikszentmihaly, a well-known psychologist and author of *Flow*, has researched in this area for more than two decades and arrived at an interesting conclusion. Happiness does not lie in mindless hedonism, but in mindful challenge. Passive, inert and leisure activities like watching TV, eating out or buying trendy outfits might give us a lot of pleasure but not necessarily enhance our happiness quotient. For that we need more of optimal experiences which Csikszentmihaly calls 'flow', where we are able to match our skills to a challenge. For example, think of the exhilaration you might have felt while trekking up a tough mountain slope, or making a brilliant presentation, or decorating your home. Flow is a feeling of transcendence when we lose sense of time and get completely absorbed into the activity.

- A series of studies conducted by Martin Seligman, pioneer of the Positive Psychology movement, found another interesting fact about happiness. There is an undeniable correlation between altruism and happiness, determining that those who believe themselves to be the happiest are also more altruistic. Close your eyes and remember the last time you opened your heart and were kind to somebody and then feel the gentle warmth of that memory envelope you. A good heart can give us happiness.

- Studies indicate that 50 per cent of our happiness is determined by our genes, 40 per cent by circumstances and 10 per cent by our intentional activity. That 10 per cent (though I personally believe it is more) is the skills that I can develop to make myself happy. That 10 per cent could also impact the 40 per cent of circumstances to tip the happiness in our favour no matter what genes we are born with. That is the reason that the studies indicate that it is not that successful people are happier but happy people are more successful. Our children learn to be happy not by being urged by us to be happy but by watching how we choose happiness no matter what. A child who watches his mother take life in her stride and continue to be happy and optimistic, despite being handicapped by an accident, is learning a most empowering life skill.

- As a parent, we love to see our children happy. So sometimes we get stuck in this pattern of doing whatever we can to make them happy. We feel if we cannot make them happy then we have failed as parents. However, we really can't make anybody happy, even if we love him or her so much. Happiness is a personal choice and a personal responsibility. So, if my daughter is looking a little low, I can spend time with her, listen to her or even suggest we do things she enjoys. However, it is important that I do not take it as my responsibility to make her happy. That is something she has to do for herself. Similarly, I can't hold other people responsible for my happiness. Happiness is a choice I have to make.

'Happiness is a way of interpreting the world, since while it may be difficult to change the world, it is always possible to change the way we look at it.'

—Matthieu Ricard, French Buddhist monk and
author of *Happiness: A Guide to Developing Life's Most
Important Skill*

Self-love and Self-compassion

I do believe that only if we love ourselves can we love others. We can't give to our children what we don't have. When we come from a position of wholeness or 'I am worthy as I am', we don't need the children to complete us. So, if you are not nurturing or loving yourself then you are not really in a position to love your children. I see this in a lot of mothers who have made being a parent the single-most important mission in their life. From the time the child gets up in the morning till he sleeps, she is at it. Feeding, fretting, changing, bathing, massaging, cajoling, coaxing, threatening, demanding, hitting, caressing, singing lullabies, requesting, shouting and collapsing to start the cycle yet again the next morning. She is at every beck and call of the child. Children stop seeing their mothers as separate human beings with their own needs and wishes. It's not much of a surprise when the mothers start complaining that their children take them for granted. Remember, you need to treat yourself the way you want them to treat you.

This kind of intensive parenting, which has also been termed as 'helicopter parenting', can be quite damaging for the parents and children. The intensive parenting approach believes that mothers are the best people to take care of their children and that the mother's life's sole purpose should be only taking care of her children.

Intensive parenting generally comes hand in hand with a perfectionist approach. 'I have to be a perfect parent' and 'I have to be the best parent'. This also means that these mothers have to have 'perfect children' and 'best children'. I remember a mother who had left her high-profile job in a company to bring up her son. She told me how she had charted out a daily schedule for her son, which included three after-school activities – swimming, piano and chess. Not only that, she also proudly told me that while ferrying him from one class to another she always played Mozart in the car which was supposed to build mathematical ability! And her son was just four!

Research indicates that laid-back mothers are happier than mothers who follow an intensive parenting model. This mother of the four year old had come to see me for depression. Apart from my initial annoyance, my heart really went out to her. When I asked her how she was taking care of herself, she broke down. She had no space for that in her life. Like all other tiger moms, she had decided that her single role in life was parenting and she was doing it with all her heart. As we worked together, I helped her see that parenting was just one aspect of her identity. The most important person in her life had to be herself. She learned to let go of her guilt and self-blame and enjoy her life more. She reconnected with her hobbies, her friends, rekindled the romance with her husband and slowly recovered from the 'perfectionist virus'.

So spare yourself all the fretting, worrying and guilting (special verb I have for mothers). It's all right, you do not have to be perfect and you can mess up at times. Parenting is not a race. Pause, take a deep breath and just let it be.

Mindfulness

The 'monkey mind' chatters away constantly, non-stop. We live from moment to moment, hour to hour, day to day in the haze of mindlessness of this constant chatter. You could be viewing the most beautiful sunset, in the most scenic setting in the mountains, but if your mind is chattering at that time, then you might as well have been sitting in your living room and watching a movie. 'Should I take a photo of this?' 'I wonder if there is any network here, then maybe I could post it on Facebook.' 'Let me check my emails and see what mails I have got.' This mindless chatter stops us from really living in the moment and experiencing our lives completely.

To top it all, we live in a day and age in which we have to multitask. You might be helping your child with her homework, supervising the dinner being cooked in the kitchen at the same time and also coaxing the other child to clear up and go for a bath. We also live in a world of constant connectivity, so in between all this you could be answering your friend's texts or shooting a few important emails from your smartphone. Research is unequivocally indicating that multitasking can not only cause huge stress, but it is not really effective as all that you are doing is dividing and diluting your attention in multiple tasks.

Mindfulness is about slowing down our minds and becoming more mindful of our internal and external world. It is about becoming aware and stepping back from the constant chatter of endless thoughts. It is about freeing our mental space so that there is more space for being present and experiencing the joy of every moment. I believe that mindfulness is an essential tool for de-stressing and being in touch with our own inner wisdom. I have found that it helps me reach a state of inner stillness that helps me be more non-reactive, more clear in my thinking and connect more deeply with my children.

Mindfulness is a daily practice. We have to slowly and

steadily weave it into our lives. You could be brushing your teeth, taking a shower, cooking, driving to work, eating your lunch, you could do it anywhere. There is no complex technique or strategy behind it – all that you have to do is become aware of your body and breathing. It is what Thich Nhat Hanh, the Zen Buddhist master described as 'coming back home to your body'. I loved a beautiful metaphor he gave to explain this process of coming back to the body. Suppose, you are sitting in a room with the windows open and suddenly a strong wind comes and blows all your papers away. You might try to chase after the papers but that does not really help. What you need to do is to close the windows first. Mindfulness is about extricating ourselves from the constant chatter and the reactivity (the wind) to bring calm and peace to ourselves.

Initially, it might be difficult so you might have to find specific times to try it out. I would suggest you start with just ten minutes every morning. Make sure all the electronic devices are mute or switched off. You could be just sitting, gardening, painting or drawing (start with a solitary peaceful activity first). Keep your attention on your breathing and your body. If thoughts come, observe them but do not engage with them. Go back to your breathing and body.

After you have done this for a few days, you can try doing it with your children around. Play with them, chat with them, laugh with them, be totally present in the moment. When the monkey mind throws its usual chatter, observe it, do not engage and go back to paying attention to your breathing and being present with your children.

You might think I am being too enthusiastic about it, yes, you are right. It has changed my life and I have enough research to back me on this to indicate that mindfulness lowers blood pressure, cortisol levels (stress hormones), increases immune responses and can also help in rewiring of the brain. I am sure we need no research to tell us what it can do to our parenting too.

Meditation

'Meditation is offering your genuine presence to yourself in every moment.'

—Thich Nhat Hanh, Zen Buddhist Master

For me, meditation and mindfulness are almost one and the same thing. When I am mindful, then I am meditative too. When I am sitting and meditating, then I am being mindful too. However, the reason I am putting it down separately is that at times it is helpful to keep some time aside for meditation. The kind when we sit alone in a quiet room, away from all distractions. Read the steps below and then try them out.

1. You do not have to sit in a lotus position (great if you can do it and it works for you), but just find a comfortable position with a back support (we mums need it) and close your eyes.

2. First of all, just focus on your breathing. There is no need to make it deep and slow, just breathe very naturally and in time you will notice that it will slow down.

3. One thing that really helps me in meditating is what Eckhart Tolle calls 'feeling your body from inside-out'. Focus on your right foot, even with your eyes closed. Can you feel the sensations inside it? Disengage from every other part of the body and feel that sensation.

4. Once you do this on a regular basis then all that you would need to do is to close your eyes and you would get transported back to your body, away from the incessant chatter of your mind.

5. Again, as the thoughts emerge, watch them but do not engage with them. They are like the voices you are hearing but do not pay much attention to them. For example, if the voice says, 'I hope Raghav does not cry in school today,' do not fret and engage in a long conversation with it, just go back to your breathing and immerse yourself inside your body.

6. Practice this for even as short as five minutes every day (put on the timer in your phone so that you do not keep checking).

Visualization

To start with, I would suggest that you start each day with visualization. Before you start the mad rush just create your day in your mind. Picture yourself going through the typical routine of the day with your children. See yourself waking them up from their sleep, getting them ready for school, picking them up from the bus stop or spending time with them later after you return from work, helping them with their homework, having dinner, going through bedtime rituals, etc. Notice the way you connect with them, how you laugh, play and have fun with them and what you do to make your relationship with them rich and rewarding. Observe how you effectively manage the particularly challenging situations like morning times with them. The more detailed you make it the more effective it will be. Visualize your voice, your facial expressions, your children's reaction, what would you be saying to each other and how the day would move smoothly and happily. And then spring out of bed lightly and make it happen.

Many of you might want to shrug this off as that new-age stuff. Some of the hot-selling best-sellers are all about the secret mantra of 'visualize and it will materialize'! But I am talking about it from my experience as a psychologist and therapist. Visualization as a technique has been used in therapy for a long time and enough research has been done on it to give it credibility in scientific journals.

To illustrate, I will give you another example. Suppose you feel you have been stuck in this negative pattern with your children when all you have been doing with them lately has been nagging, pushing and ordering. It has drained you out and most days you get up feeling a sense of dread which makes you feel, 'Oh no! I can't go through another of those mornings.'

- I would ask you to find a quiet place, close your eyes and visualize yourself going through the typical routine of the morning. Where most mornings you might have been rushed, irritable, critical, shouting and threatening, this

morning you visualize yourself to be very calm, playful,
loving and unruffled. Visualize how you would wake the
children up a little earlier so that you have enough time
to gently hug and kiss them and wish them a cheery good
morning. Picture how you would maybe keep chatting to
them as you put on some of their favourite music. As they
doddle and whinge (kids are going to be kids), you tickle
them, laugh out loud, joke playfully, pull them out of bed
and get them started. As you get their breakfast ready,
imagine yourself humming a song happily or chatting to
your spouse. As they make their way to the breakfast table,
see how you would read out bits from the newspaper to
them. Finally, you would see them off with a warm hug
and head back to start your daily routine.

- The more detailed you make it the more effective it will
  be. Visualize the clothes you would be wearing, the smile
  on your face, the light in the room, what music you would
  play, what would be there for breakfast, what sounds
  would be there in the house. Imagine your children and
  how they would initially protest but, then, 'pulled' by
  your warmth, how they would reciprocate with a smile
  or maybe even chat about something they were looking
  forward to that day. Visualize your voice, your facial
  expressions, every step or gesture you make. Focus more
  on yourself rather than others. As I have already stressed,
  it is about the 'inside-out' focus.

- You might not have time to do this visualization in detail
  every day but do it once in a while when you feel you
  are getting stuck in a negative loop in any aspect of your

life and maybe revisit it once for a minute or two every morning and see how it works like magic.

So how does something as simple as this really work?

- **Brain trainer**: Visualization opens up our brain to new possibilities. It primes the brain and creates neural pathways. Behavioural and imaging studies suggest that when humans mentally rehearse a familiar action they execute some of the same neural operations used during overt motor performance. No wonder visualization is a crucial part of athletic training for Olympics in what is known as Visual Motor Behaviour Rehearsal (VMBR). Michael Phelps, winner of 22 Olympic medals in swimming, is well known for using visualization as a core training strategy.

- **Creativity enhancer**: Visualization activates the creative sub-conscious, which generates ideas and ingenuity. Like a painter who stares into space for hours capturing the picture in her mind's eye before transferring it on to the canvas.

- **Energizer and motivator**: At times we get so overwhelmed with the daily stress that life gets restricted to a pillar-to-post existence. And when we think about bringing about a change we often get into a 'push mode'. This pushing can drain out a lot of energy and slowly wash out motivation. It seems like such a drag. On the other hand, visualization works on 'pull mode'. Once we have visualized something, it pulls us towards itself with an astonishing energy.

Eat, Move, Sleep

A lot has been written, there has been a lot of research, but the three simple gems of health are sleeping well, eating right and moving a lot! I am not a super health enthusiast but over the years I have started valuing and realizing that the quality of my life depends mainly on how much I take care of my health. Also, only if I take care of my health will I be able to be there for my kids as they grow older.

- **Eat**: I know the nutrition and diet industry is churning out more books, magazines and diet plans by the day but to me it is pretty simple. Eat healthy, eat small portions, eat on time and eat slowly. Since each person has a different need and metabolism, there is no 'one size fits all' in eating patterns too.
- **Move**: Tom Rath, in his book *Eat, Move, Sleep* (from where I borrow my subtitle) says that research indicates sitting to be the biggest health hazard. As I read somewhere, 'Sitting is the New Smoking'! All electric activity is cut to the legs when we sit, calories we burn drastically come down to one per minute and enzyme production also dips by 90 per cent. So keep moving, even if your work demands long hours sitting in front of the computer, keep getting up, do some stretches, move around and shake it a little. Health experts say that we need to take 10,000 steps a day. Most people average around 2,500 a day. I wear a fitness band to make sure that I keep track of my steps. It's funny but having that little ticking device can really help you be more mindful and keep moving. You might want to

brush this aside with a, 'I go to the gym three days a week, so I don't need to do all this.' Well, you will be surprised to hear that studies have indicated that your movements through the day are much more important than just three hours of vigorous exercises through the week.

- **Sleep:** As I am growing older, I am realizing that sleep is the single-most dealmaker and deal-breaker for me. I know that if I started sleeping a little earlier, the quality of my life would change dramatically. This is one bad habit I have struggled with most of my lifetime. I love the quiet of the night when everybody has gone off to sleep and I can just snuggle in my bed and read. Just reaching out and switching off the bedside lamp is really a struggle for me. I have learned to overcome this habit (all right, let me admit it that I still slip up most times) by preparing for bed much earlier than I used to. Research has even calculated the amount of sleep you need in a day – eight hours and 36 minutes. So try to get those few cat-naps here and there if you can't get them at a stretch. One thing I do on most days (as I have to wake up very early to get the kids ready for school), which really helps me, is that after my yoga in the morning, I take a nap of twenty minutes, which really revives me instantly. Actually, after all these years, I have learned to sleep anywhere at any time. At times all I need is a five-minute break and I am off. All that you have to do is switch off your mind (yes, yes, you can do this with practice) and just focus on your being in your body and focus on your breathing. Try it out, it can work like magic!

Daily Journal

I have been writing a journal since I was a teenager. It has been my life's anchor, my sounding board, my alter ego. My journal time is my time to myself, to reflect, to heal and to realign myself to what I believe in. Many a times, troubles, which seemed so huge in my mind, vanish as soon as I have them in black and white. At times, it is just a line and at times I just can't seem to stop myself and keep on writing. From my experience and from what I have gathered from people who write regular journals, there are three elements to a journal. Dumping and unburdening of troubles, difficulties, dilemmas, pain, then reconnecting with your priorities and guideposts in life, finally, ending on a hopeful note of the way forward or 'this is what I am going to do'. You might despair that you don't want to add another task to your already heavy scheduling but give it a try. Even a simple – 'Got up in the morning in a fog of funk. Guess the negative thoughts are having a field day. I choose happiness today. An extra dose of laughter, hugs, exercise is what I need.' If you don't want to write then there are some amazing apps like Day One that are designed really well.

Dance Like Nobody is Watching

Mark Twain said, 'Dance like no one is watching. Sing like no one is listening.' For me playfulness is to let myself be silly, crazy, spontaneous and mad. In our grown-up world, it seems a little ridiculous to talk about playfulness. It sounds frivolous, juvenile and silly. However, I feel that playfulness needs to be at the core of who we are as people and how we live our lives. I believe that our playfulness quotient (PQ: a term I have coined myself, as mentioned earlier) is a single determinant of our quality of life. I have a deal with my children. Whenever they feel that they are losing me to the adult serious world that they cannot connect to they immediately remind me, 'Mum, please check your PQ level.'

Building PQ

- **Body talk:** We carry a lot of grown-upness as inhibited stiffness in our bodies. So try letting your body go and feel yourself come alive. Roll up your sleeves, loosen that tie and kick off those heels. Crawl with your toddler, jive with your teenager, shake a leg, kick the ball, splash in the pool or goof around in the local park. Anything as long as it has no hidden agenda (I need to lose weight, I have to improve my dancing skills). The only agenda you have to stick to at that time is having fun.
- **Hearty laugh:** Try a little exercise. Just laugh out aloud. You will find it a little artificial initially but then you will suddenly feel it coming more naturally. Notice how your whole body and mind suddenly feels injected with refreshing energy. Studies have indicated that when we use our facial muscles to express emotions, we trigger specific happy hormones.
- **Be silly:** We have grown up hearing 'Don't be silly' for so many years that to do the opposite might be a little tough

at first. However, do not give up. Belt out the Bollywood number while giving your little one a shower, give yourself and your child 'silliness breaks' during homework time, play hopscotch, go and give everyone at home a bear hug. Just like that. And feel the years slipping away, leaving you invigorated and ready to face life.

• **PQ reminders:** I remember when my daughter was little, she used to do something which acted as an amazing PQ reminder for me. Whenever I was sitting deep in thought, oblivious to the world and her, she would come very close to my face and give me a big smile. I would immediately smile at her and feel the weight of the world lift from my shoulders. To kick-start the playful makeover, I would suggest that you put PQ reminders for yourself. Plan regular playful breaks during your hectic schedule. Let the red light be a time not to curse the traffic but to get in touch with hidden singing talent. Most of all, let your children, the real fun experts, help you to stay on the playful track. Initially it will be tough but with time it will come easily.

'We don't stop playing because we grow old; we grow old because we stop playing.'
　　　　　　—George Bernard Shaw, author and playwright

There is an amazing body of evidence which indicates that playfulness decreases the stress hormones like cortisol, nor epinephrine or what we call adrenaline. On the other hand, it increases happiness chemicals such as endorphins and immune-boosting cells, lowering blood pressure, relaxing muscles, reducing pain and accelerating healing. Another interesting fact is that we connect much more deeply and meaningfully to people when we are playful. The healthy dose of happy hormones like oxytocin and serotonin can nurture and strengthen bonds for life. So laugh, dance, sing, be crazy, whacky and silly.

Forgiveness

There is something very exciting about the recent research in the area of forgiveness. What the Eastern spiritual practices have always believed, the Western science is now proving through research. It is becoming clear that forgiveness is the key to spiritual, psychological and physical health. So, if you have been nurturing a grudge against somebody for sometime, then maybe it is time for you to let it go. It might be the healthiest decision you might make in your life.

I remember a mother I met a few years ago who had to leave her successful career due to debilitating dizziness spells. It transpired that as a child she had been severely bullied by her older sister. At a crucial juncture in therapy, I checked with her if she was ready to forgive her estranged sister. Though she dismissed my query, she came back the following week looking visibly at peace. After some deliberation she had sent a 'forgiveness email' to her sister. She promptly got a warm reply and suddenly felt the 'years of bitterness fading away'. However, what was most amazing was that there was a remarkable decline in her dizziness spells and soon she resumed work!

Admittedly, not all recoveries are so sensational. At times, the process of forgiveness might take a little longer. After all, we have nursed these grudges for months and years and letting go of them might not be so easy. According to research, unforgiving people are prone to cardiovascular problems, chronic back pain, impaired neurological functioning, suppressed immunity, anxiety and depression. Not to mention lack of social networking as every grudge is hoarded and nurtured till the world seems hostile.

Forgiveness research also highlights an interesting dimension as far as gender differences are concerned. Women are more likely to forgive than men, but both are equal in seeking revenge. That might be the reason that more women try to kiss and make up after a fight but will run themselves down to get even if they are deeply hurt.

Forgiveness Skills

Personally I can say from my own experience that building my forgiveness skills has been very liberating. I feel much more at peace with my family, friends and colleagues. For this forgiveness should be incorporated into our way of life, our daily practice and not merely as a response to specific insults.

- Breathe softly and scan your mind for any resentment you are keeping locked in. Visualize it as a tight knot holding you down. Breathe into it slowly and deeply. Now imagine it slowly melting away and leaving you feeling light and free. Some people find visualizing a white light around it and dissolving the knot into thin air very effective. Be mindful of any thoughts that come up and let them go gently. Forgiveness does not always mean reconciliation. It is not about excusing or condoning the other person's behaviour but about letting go off your own suffering.

- If there is a deep-seated hostility towards somebody from the past, then writing a forgiveness letter to the person might help. If you do not want to mail it then burn it away and imagine your feeling of revenge disappearing too. For some people, the feeling is the same though the persons who are causing it might be different. A daily ritual of writing forgiveness notes might be a useful safety valve.

- Remember, it takes all kind of people to make up this world. There might be people who can be insensitive, inconsiderate and abusive. That is the way they choose to be in their relationships. They might not know any other way. However, do not let their negative vibes rub off on you. Move to a higher level of being. Keep the energy around you free and uncontaminated.

The message is clear. Spurn it rather than churn in it.

Anti-perfectionism

Is the word 'perfectionist' used for you quite often? It could have even be used as a compliment by a few and you might have accepted it with pride. As a reformed perfectionist, I can confess, that there was a time I used to be a stickler for my training workshops. I would sit for hours 'perfecting' my presentation, churning inside and in the end not really finding any joy in training others. It was as if I had this 'inspector' sitting on my shoulder telling me no matter how much I tried that I was not meeting this imagined standard. It took me some time to realize that I was actually making my work a burden by obsessing about perfecting it.

Let me clarify that there is a difference between being a 'perfectionist' and being 'in the flow'. Let us say a person is throwing a party for her friends and spends hours shopping for groceries, cooking and decorating. She would be in the flow if she really enjoyed doing so – losing track of time and really immersing herself in the process. On the other hand, it would be perfectionism if she got herself really worked up, exhausting herself with some unrealistic standard of what 'should be' or the 'right thing to do'. The former would enrich and deepen her experiences and relationships and the latter would turn into a burden of perfecting, performing and pleasing others.

I read about an interesting story about a pottery class in a book by Bayles & Orland (*Art and Fear*). Students were divided into two groups – the first group was told that they would be evaluated on the basis of the quantity/weight of the pots they created. The second group was told that they had two days to make one perfect pot!

What do you think happened? Which group do you think was most creative? Which group do you think had the most fun? The first one, of course! I am sure they played, they laughed, they created, they made a mess, they broke and then they started all over again. I am not sure what really happened to the second group. But I can just imagine their frustration, competitiveness and the furtive looks they were giving one another to check how they were progressing as they all worked to create their masterpiece.

Inoculating against the Perfectionist Virus

- Be alert to this virus: It creeps up on us so stealthily that we are not even aware of it at most times. Remember, its two steady friends are guilt and anxiety. So, if you do not get everything ticked off from the list, everyday, you could feel the sense of uneasiness, maybe a restlessness, sleeplessness and a voice of the 'inspector' urging you, 'not good enough, you have to try harder'.

- Label the culprit: Rather than feeling guilty, label the voice as the perfectionist virus and see it slowly melt away. Just that sense of detachment with the attitude of 'it's not me but the perfectionist virus' can work wonders at putting you more at ease.

- Keep at it: Like any training, it will take you a little while to get used to this way of life. I have to admit that even now, before every training workshop, I get a call from this virus and a combination of 'So what?' and 'What will be the worst-case scenario?' helps me stay on track. This approach has helped me stay relaxed, be more creative and get more joy out of my work.

Every time you feel the perfectionist virus creep up on you, take a deep breath and tell yourself, 'I am going to focus on making this process joyful rather than perfect!'

Creativity

I have heard many people say, 'I am not the creative type' but I have always wondered if it is true. I think each one of us, deep down, is very creative. Children start being creative from the time they are little. They love to draw, colour, paint, make fun stuff with play dough, build, construct with blocks, 'cook' and what not. It's only as they grow older that we start telling them to stop messing around, be neat, colour between the lines and create what their teachers ask them to. That's where we start losing it. Very soon kids start getting the message that there are only a few 'artistic' kids in the class, the ones who make very neat drawings, colour between the lines, paint neatly and copy what they are told. The rest take to hiding their untidy drawings, messy paintings and unwieldy projects. By the time they are in senior school they give it up completely. I was one of those kids and it was only when my kids were small that I rekindled my pleasure in just messing around with drawings, colouring and painting. It was quite recently that I discovered the amazing meditative art form called Zentangling. There might be many who might dismiss it as 'not really a true art form' but I can spend hours doing it as I find it extremely healing and relaxing. So discover your art form – it could be anything from painting, drawing, sketching, doodling, paper-cutting, origami, garden landscaping, Zentangling, decorating, collaging, photography, making movies, sculpting, scrapbooking, dancing, acting or singing. Just go and do it. Keep some time every day, or every weekend for it. Smile at people who tell you to stop fooling around and wasting your time, stick your tongue out to your perfectionist virus and have fun. Make it a priority. You were born to be an artist too.

Gratitude

There would be a time when I would not even have touched this concept with a bargepole. It was too new-agey and airy-fairy for me. Even when I started going through the research on it, it took me a long time to get my head around it. But now I feel that it is an essential part of who I am and also a part of my daily practice. I do not think gratitude is something you have or not, it is something you need to do, everyday. As Brené Brown has pointed out in her book, joy and gratitude go together. Right now I am sitting in my balcony on a beautiful day. All around me I can see stretches of lush green trees, broken by the gorgeous red of the bottle brush. The sound of the birds (in the past one hour I have already spotted a barbet, a bee-eater and several tree-pies), scurrying of the squirrels and distant laughter of the kids playing in the park is giving me a rare moment of peace and inner stillness. Inside the house I can hear my daughter playing the guitar and my son singing on the top of his voice. If I describe my feeling then it is immense gratitude and due to that – pure joy. I have developed this daily practice of going through my day every night and observing gratitude. It might seem a little silly and artificial but I can tell you that I love gathering the golden nuggets that, otherwise, would have been forgotten in the rush of life. It could range from a meaningful therapy session, to a warm chat with a friend, a walk in the park with my children to a delicious dinner cooked by my husband. Like a magpie, I store all my 'shiny moments' in the treasure chest. There are days when these moments overwhelm me and there are days when I barely manage to scrounge around any. And that is fine too as tomorrow is another day!

Rhythm and Daily Practice

Living my life in rhythm gives me peace. Without being too structured I like to make sure that I find time for all that I am passionate about. Family, work, health, home, writing, reflections, reading and music all flow in a cadence if I am able to follow a certain rhythm of life between doing and being.

One of the biggest obstacles to building rhythm is embedded in unhealthy habits. Our deeply entrenched habits make it very difficult for us to change. They are programmed in our brain and tightly wired into our day-to-day lives. Many times, when we struggle to change or fail, we lash out at ourselves for not having enough willpower. Imagine willpower to be a little reservoir that we need to dip in every time we try to break a habit. In his fascinating book, *Thinking Fast and Slow*, Nobel prize winner Daniel Kahneman uses the metaphor of electricity to explain the mental energy or willpower required to do something effortful. Small changes are like switching on a light bulb, which are not a big drain on the electric supply. However, sudden big changes are like switching on an air conditioner, which can completely deplete our supply.

For example, if I get up an hour earlier than my usual time, I have made a big dip into my willpower and then if, unlike my usual routine, I go for a brisk morning walk, I dip some more into my willpower pool. By the time it is time for breakfast, my willpower has got depleted further (what the researchers called ego depletion) and I settle down for a heavy breakfast of buttery toast, omelette and bacon, though I had planned on just muesli (I have no more willpower left to put on the AC). I also justify it to myself that I need it for all the effort I have put in. I might be able to carry it out for a few days but then I get depleted with all the withdrawal from the mental energy and stop. I tell myself, it is too difficult, I am not a morning person, I need more sleep and that's that.

Keeping this metaphor in mind, suppose I start with baby steps. I begin by exercising for ten minutes. I make it a daily practice just like brushing my teeth and taking a shower. I start small, make it regular and before you know it, it is part of my daily life. It gets wired into my brain and as it does not require too much effort, I do not feel so threatened. Like most other daily activities, it is not a drain on my reserve as my brain has already got programmed to do it effortlessly. It is like switching on a bulb and not an AC.

I read somewhere that the worth of your day depends on the quality of your mornings. I would grudgingly agree with this as despite not being much of a morning person in the past, I feel that my morning rituals have changed the quality of my life. After I have sent the kids to school, I spend some time on my own doing my daily rituals – meditating, writing my journal, planning the day, exercising and finally getting ready. At night, before sleeping, I do go through my day and feel deep gratitude for all that is wonderful in my life. I have even managed to write this book through this daily ritual practice! I even have five minutes of de-cluttering time every day in the morning. So rather than wait for one day when I will have a full day to clear up the rubbish in the house (which we know will never happen), I just keep squirrelling five minutes a day. Every part of my life I have turned into a daily ritual. Of course, there are days when I skip these because I have got up late, I am short of time or I am just lazy.

I would suggest that you build a flow of core activities you have to do every morning and call it the power hour. It will not be easy at first (One research has even mentioned the need for 66 days to establish a new habit!), but keep going and you will be amazed at how much you will be able to achieve in a single day. It is the small changes that can bring about significant ones. As Gretchen Rubin, author of *Happiness Project* put it, 'What I do everyday matters more than what I do once in a while.'

'A small daily task, if it really be daily, will beat the labour of a spasmodic Hercules.'

—Anthony Trollope, English novelist

'We are what we repeatedly do. Excellence then is not an act but a habit.'

—Aristotle, philosopher

Flipping the Energy

I believe that at any given time, we are either connected to our lower or higher self. The lower self lives in an impoverished, contracted, negative state. It wallows in feeling unworthy and victimized, being petty, angry, irritable, blaming, shaming, complaining, being competitive, resentful, bitter, envious, jealous, critical, judgemental, vicious, inadequate, fearful, victimized and seeking love rather than giving it. On the other hand, our higher self lives in a positive state and it comes from a position of being luminous, joyous, at peace, loving, open-hearted, caring, giving, generous, confident, worthy, courageous, authentic, celebrating others, forgiving, not judgemental, accepting, serene, contented, accepting of 'what is', respectful of the self and others. It comes from a position of acceptance, love and wisdom. Our lower self drains us whereas our higher self makes us complete, energizes us and sets us free.

ABC Approach to Flipping the Energy

Alert: It takes a lot of courage and honesty to be able to acknowledge our lower self. However, it is absolutely essential we do so to be able to access our higher self. If you are a regular practitioner of mindfulness, this will happen effortlessly. So, watch out for each and every worrying, nagging, self-pitying, self-doubting, brooding, critical, moaning, angry and complaining feeling. Do not resist it or engage with it but just observe it. After years of meditation and mindfulness, it has become very natural for me to become aware of my lower self. I can sense it in my body and in my thoughts. My jaws tighten and I can feel a tightness in my chest. My mind starts racing with, 'How dare they?' 'I will not accept this,' or maybe, 'I will never be able to do this, it is hopeless.' I have observed that as soon as I have acknowledged these feelings they slowly start disappearing.

Breathe: Take a long deep breath, exhale and then inhale. Breathe out through your mouth and breathe in through your nose. Fill your lungs with oxygen and let it slowly relax every part of your body, breathing out every bit of tension.

Change the channel: Gently release the grip of your lower self and let it go by slowly making space for positive energy in your life. Open your heart to all people and things you love, visualize a scene or an experience that leaves you energized. Start connecting to all the feelings that come with our higher self – gratitude, generosity, joy, hope, peace and love. Experience these feelings at a cellular level till your whole being is pulsating with energy.

As Rumi describes the lower self as guests from the dark side, *'This being human is a guest house, every morning a new arrival. The dark thought, the sane, the shame, the malice, meet them at the door laughing and invite them in. Be grateful for whoever comes, because each guest has been sent as a guide from beyond.'*

Flipping the energy might seem a little difficult at first but with practice it will become something you might access and amplify anytime during the day. Some days it will come out gushing, flooding every cell of your being and at times a drop or two might just trickle out. That's fine, just stay in tune with the reservoir within you that needs no words, no conditions to make you reach the highest version of yourself. All you need to do is to move to that space of wordlessness and get in touch with the immense pool of joy and wisdom within you.

Reflection

1. What are the three things that you can adopt as daily practice, which will change your life? Remember, start with baby steps so even five minutes on each would be fine.
2. How can you try to build an internal witness, which lets you stay mindful and not get lost in mindless chatter?
3. Think of one artistic activity, no matter how silly or bizarre, you will do to connect to your creativity?
4. What is one thing you will do to notch up your PQ on a daily basis?
5. Of the fourteen practices highlighted in this chapter, which three would you like to start with?

5

COMMUNITY

'It takes a village to raise a child.'

—African proverb

*W*e are hardwired to seek connections, to love, to be loved and to belong. A child who grows up in a home, a family, a neighbourhood and a school with a sense of belonging has already got a head start in life. She has grown up with 'I am loved, I am welcomed and I belong' and carries a deep sense of security and well-being that can act as the buffer to help her face the worst knocks in her life. On the other hand, a child who grows up with 'I am not sure if I am loved or wanted' can grow up with a very different feeling. She would go through life wondering, doubting and desperately trying to fit in. There is a big difference in belonging and fitting in. When you have a sense of belonging, you know deep down that you are accepted as you are. Whereas, when you are trying to fit in then you feel that you have to act in a certain way. Only then will you be accepted.

For each of us there are spaces where we feel a greater sense of belonging. Where we can be ourselves and our flaws, eccentricities, quirks and craziness will be accepted. Those are the spaces that we seek and where we feel energized and rejuvenated. They give us a greater sense of rootedness and connection. It could be our families, friends, workspaces, etc. It could be people who we meet and connect with due to our common interest or to build our sense of family. Football leagues in Europe, the worldwide camaraderie of wild-lifers, birdwatchers and environmentalists are perfect examples of connect.

There are spaces where we know that we won't be accepted for who we are. We would be criticized, judged, shamed and ridiculed. At times blatantly and at times in a most subtle form that slowly eats into our own sense of self-worth. I am sure we have all had that experience when we have walked into a social gathering where we had to really put in a lot of effort to fit in, in terms of the way we dressed, talked and acted.

What if a child had to live in that space for a large part of her life? Sue Monk Kid, author of *When the Heart Waits*, puts it as a trinity of Ps – Pleasing, Performing and Perfecting – the only acts that will guarantee her acceptance in this world provided she adopts them. What does that do to a child's growth as a person and build a sense of authenticity and sense of 'I am worthy and I like myself as I am'. There are a large number of children who grow with that sense of not belonging and desperately trying to fit in. Where they are not accepted for who they are due to their gender, disability, intellect, class, caste, race, cultural background and looks.

These are children who, in their families – extended and joint – carry the narrative of not being good enough. They are rejected, ignored and mocked for being who they are. They are compared to their sisters, brothers, cousins and found lacking. They grow up lurking in the shadows and dark corners with a sense of being a burden on their families and not being 'good enough'.

I grew up in a small town in the hills, which valued itself on 'everybody knows everybody'. My home extended to many other homes of my friends and relatives where I would spend my time. My friends and I felt that we owned the expanse of the town and beyond. We had named our favourite mountaintops and the trees where we spent our afternoons chatting, reading books and finishing our homework. My holidays were spent in my grandmother's village where there were just four or five families living within a distance of half a kilometre from each other. The daily rhythm of my grandmother milking the cows at the crack of dawn, making fresh butter which my brother and I would have for breakfast and then setting out with the women and children to work in the fields will be etched in my mind forever. An early lunch was followed by a game of cricket, gulli danda and then joining the village kids as they foraged for wood in the forest for the chulha to be lit to cook dinner. Our lives were lived outside the home and the sense of community was strong. Though I came from a more privileged background, it never got in the way of our relationship. They marvelled at the way I could speak English and read piles of books and I marvelled at their skill in tending the cattle and the speed with which they could build a haystack. I have grown and wandered away but I still carry that village with me wherever I go. I really wish my children had a 'village' that they could carry with them.

Children need their villages and they crave desperately for them. In the present age, as we have been unable to provide it to them, they have sought it in the form of Facebook,

Twitter, Instagrams and Snapchats. Every 'like' on these social media forums is like a validation of their visibility and existence. More invisible the children are, higher is their need for visibility and acceptance. Adolescents who have gone through years of rejection, neglect and abuse are more attracted to gangs where they feel they would be accepted for who they are. Human beings are cognitively, emotionally, neurologically and spiritually wired to seek a sense of belonging. We pursue membership of our families, school, workplace, friend circle, neighbourhood, religion, culture and country. In our fast-paced, instant, expressway world we are somehow losing the essence of the community. I see so many families where the only caring adults that the child has access to are his parents (who he might only see in the evenings and weekends), maybe a single parent and, if they are lucky, a nurturing and committed teacher. We do not even think there is anything wrong with that, as that has become the reality of most urban families and a norm.

This is not a call to go back to a joint family system or people taking to living only in towns and cities where they have their families. I just think we need to actively look at ways to build nurturing ecosystems for our children. I have a strong belief that if a child has more people strongly committed to his rearing in his life, he will grow up to be more stronger, confident and secure.

We have to build communities that are worthy of our children. Not just for some children but for each and every child. An essential mark of an evolved society is how they take care of their children. In our country, we have a long way to go to achieve anything close to that. This is not a responsibility we must leave to the government, the bureaucrats who define policies or to a handful of NGOs that are doing great work in this field. Each one of us has to work at seeing how we can make it a better world for them. Though extremely critical, addressing issues of street children, children impacted by trauma and deprivation will be beyond the scope of this book. I will focus on how we can take care of the children in our regular families and communities. As Daniel Coleman, author of *Emotional Inteligence*, puts it: 'Our relationships in the community are like emotional vitamins nourishing us for an optimal human existence.'

Home

Our homes need to be like sanctuaries where children can be given space just to be who they are. Where they can be accepted with all their frailties and weaknesses. They need to know that at home they can express their frustrations, annoyances, anger, irritation, troubles, fears, jealousies and insecurities and it would not be criticized or suppressed. Most importantly, they need to know that home is one place where they can be vulnerable, where they would not be attacked for their imperfections. They need to know that at home they can say, 'I don't know' or that 'I messed up' without their parents coming down on them like a ton of bricks.

They also need a sense of ownership to get a stronger sense of belonging. It could be their own rooms or their own corners, cupboards, shelves or walls, where they are allowed to do what they want. As they get older, the need for private space grows, so let them shut their door and respect their solitude.

Parental Relationship

Children thrive in families where their parents come together to love them and draw clear boundaries for them. They also need parents who share a loving, caring and respectful relationship with each other. Constant conflicts, cold silences and a hostile environment can be extremely damaging for children. As a young girl, who had witnessed too many fights at home, tearfully shared with me in therapy, 'Every day, as I return from school, I am scared to enter my house as I don't know how the atmosphere will be. There are times I wish I could just run away from home.'

Many times parents think that children are not even aware of their heated arguments as they fight in their bedrooms or when the children are sleeping. They are not aware that children do not need to witness the actual fight to know that things are not all right. Even little babies are very sensitive to the level of stress in the house. They are like sponges soaking in the internal tension and strain.

Parental conflict drains children of their life energy. They inadvertently get drawn into feeling that somehow they are to blame and they have to take sides or protect the weaker parent. Similarly, children who are shared by divorced parents generally have it very tough too. They end up becoming pawns in the bitter battles that their parents are waging on each other. Every point they score against each other also turns out to be a point against the child.

Sibling Relationship

They are our tormentors, our protectors, our playmates, our enemies, our source of annoyance and happiness, resentment and love, and jealousy and pride. Living with them annoys us no end and living without them would kill us. Confused with the paradoxes? That is what a sibling is!

If you have one then you will immediately relate to what I am talking about. I am sure you remember the days when you found it totally intolerable to even share the roof with him, when you ranted about how she should leave your things alone and how his sloppiness was so annoying. But then I am sure, you also remember the nights when you giggled endlessly under the quilt, when even a tiny piece of chocolate was shared with intense pleasure, when you spoke in a secret code nobody else on this earth could follow.

When I look at my children, I am reminded of my relationship with my older brother. The complex dance every sibling relationship has followed since eternity. She teases – he snaps; she whines – he jeers; she screams – he is questioned; she is smug – he protests. Or he provokes – she is cutting; he is sarcastic – she fights; he laughs – she is ready to pounce; he negotiates – she huffs and puffs. And what I marvel at most is the way the grudges are brushed off so lightly and the siblings are back together, thick as thieves again – laughing, joking, sharing and plotting. I watch amused and marvel at life's most important socializing lessons being played out so beautifully. They are learning to express discomfort, be assertive, deal with perceived/real parental favouritism, maintain acceptable boundaries, think on their feet, manage their anger, walk away from a non-redeemable situation and then bounce back again without an iota of rancour.

A sibling is a buffer, an oasis that soaks up your angst, frustration and conflict. He can understand you better than anyone else. She can stand up for you, be it during a playground fight, against class bullies or the lashing of an unreasonable parent. But then, they are the ones who compete with you for your primal love (your mother); where territories are drawn, marked and then infringed upon; and bitter fights raged. At times for almost a life span.

If we think about it, a sibling is the only person who shares most of our journey in life. From the first toothless smile to the last toothless one. From creation of the first dream to the fulfilment of the last one. They are with us for a lifetime.

I have always wondered what really makes the sibling relationship work and build camaraderie.

- Common threads at play: My kids are very differently wired from each other but they have many shared fantasies and passions – from Harry Potter, *Lord of the Rings*, *Star Wars*, the Batman series, theatre to conserving wild life and feeding stray puppies in the colony. Look for these common interests and nurture them even if it does not make much sense to you. This is going to be their medium to connect with each other and build a common language.
- Stay out: Siblings are also people who know you without

the masks that you put on in front of the world. They know your vulnerabilities and your imperfections like nobody else in this world. So it also very important that you make sure they learn to respect each other's vulnerabilities and not attack them in their weak moments. Comments like 'You are a loser, you have no friends' or 'You can't even read, Dyslexic' should be an absolute no-no if they end up hurting the child deeply and taking away from his sense of dignity. Recognize them every time they fight the urge to retaliate and break the pattern. However, if they are going through a phase when they can't stop harmlessly jibing at each other, just stay right out of it and you might be really surprised how quickly they sort it out.

- Be mindful of your role: Many times parents, in order to make their work easier, start pitting one child against another by making them compete against each other (Let's see who finishes the milk first!), comparing them (Why can't you listen to me like your brother does?), forming triangles (If your brother fights with you then you come and play with me!), and playing spying games (Call me if your sister is watching TV and not studying!).

- Sense of solidarity: I must admit I get peeved with the way my kids gang up against me. At times, I might be trying to have a 'firm conversation' with one of them and I see the look exchanged between them – rolling of eyes with 'there she goes again'. I have learned to live with the fact that they share much more with each other than with me. It troubles me at times but I realize that this is important for them.

Joint/Extended Families

My grandparents are part of my most treasured memories of childhood. My grandfather was particularly very involved in our lives from a very age. Life seemed like an adventure with him whether it was climbing mountains, walking through forests or listening to his stories of Krishna or his experiences of freedom fighting during bedtime. I believe that children need as many caring and loving adults in their lives as possible, be it parents, grandparents, aunts or uncles. The more they have the better it is for them.

However, what we need to watch out for is when these adults start settling their scores through children. So it could be a grandmother who, in a most subtle manner, undermines the mother's position by letting her grandson watch too much of TV. Or it could be a mother who does not let her daughter spend enough time with the grandparents to settle old scores. Children need adults who love them but also who are mature enough to put their differences aside to see what is best for the children. So I would urge parents to discuss this book with your own parents, siblings and cousins. Start a discussion on parenting and reach a consensus on what would work best for your family. When the topic does become sticky or heated just keep one question in mind, 'What would be best for our children?' Do not let interpersonal differences relating to the children's grandparents, uncles, aunts and cousins come in the way of your relationship with your kids.

Having said that, at times, families can become an adverse source of negative stories for some children. Narratives like, 'problem child' or 'not so smart as her cousins' can become very damaging for children as they are growing up. Parents need to play an active role in building a richer narrative, highlighting their children's strengths, recognizing each and every achievement and shaping the way people think about them by reframing their language. So 'stubborn' is seen as being 'determined', 'distracted' is warmly described as being a 'dreamer', 'slow' as 'likes to do things at his pace' and 'boisterous' as 'full of beans'. The other family members generally take their cue on how to describe a child from his parents. So make sure that you have a rich vocabulary to describe your child. A story is not a story till it has found an audience. So, to build richer stories about your child, which he, possibly, will carry for the rest of his life, be mindful of the words you are using. As I had mentioned earlier, along with how we talk to our children, we have to be careful about how we talk about them.

Another very important part of a family is the family stories that we pass on to our children. These stories provide a sense of belongingness to our children. As a kid I remember being riveted by my grandfather's stories. He ran away from home in the mountains when he was ten years old. His parents had died and his well-meaning older brother wanted him to discontinue studies and work in the fields. He left home and at a very early age, apart from fending for himself and studying, he also became involved in the freedom struggle. His life stories will make another book some other time but I do remember the sense of pride with which I cherished the stories. When I grew up, the freedom struggle had a personal meaning for me. Hopefully, I have passed on that connect to my kids too and the chain will go on.

The festival time is a great time to connect with our community, especially close friends and relatives. When I look back at the eight years I spent in the UK with my family, I can definitely recall the October–December festival time being really tough. We did our rounds of the Durga puja pandals, lighting the fireworks, decorating the Christmas tree and doing everything we could do to recreate the festive spirit back home. But it was never like the real thing. It was banal. The soul was missing.

Returning to India and being part of the festivities was really a true homecoming. In Indian cities, we might go through our own individual lives throughout the year but come festival time and bang, the community wakes up. It wakes up with such pageantry and ceremony that you have no option but to celebrate life and connections.

Neighbourhood

Children cannot get a sense of community sitting at home and being ferried to schools and malls in their cars. They need to walk around their neighbourhood, play in the parks, and discover the interesting corners and patches so as to feel connected to the real world. Not only does it help them have a strong sense of ownership of their world, but it also helps build their visuospatial ability and street smartness. We live in a fairly safe neighbourhood and my twelve-year-old daughter loves to explore various parks in our locality as the self-appointed caregiver of all the puppies. On one hand, I revel in her adventurous spirit but on the other I dread her tendency to spend so much time in the colony's nooks and crannies with the latest litter. However, we have reached a clear understanding about the parts of the colony she can roam about, with whom, at what time and also what steps she should take to ensure her safety. It would definitely be more convenient and reassuring for me to have her stay at home but that is not going to help her grow and get her bearings. Let them negotiate with the outside world on their own. Let your tween go and get stuff from the corner shop in your locality and let your teen take a metro ride to her friend's place. Teach them the basic safety rules and what to do in case of an emergency and let them be on their own.

I know we are constantly worrying about how unsafe the world is for women and children. Safety is not about overprotecting our children and keeping them away from danger at any cost. It is about preparing them for the world and making them worldly wise. It is about making them stronger physically through self-defense classes and preparing them mentally for any high-risk situation. We have to get our heads out of the sand and realize that possible abuse is a reality for any child and that should make us all the more determined to train them every step of the way.

You could take on different projects in your neighbourhood. They could be taking care of the puppies and dogs, de-littering the park, growing a flower patch, educating children from underprivileged backgrounds, making Diwali pollution free, or having a garage sale for charity. Thanks to my daughter and her neighbourhood friends, we have tried all of them at different times and they have been great fun and hugely enriching.

Schools

Visualize a school where each and every child is valued. Where from the time he joins the school till the time he leaves, he is given a clear message, 'You are worthy as you are'. Where children are not discriminated on the basis of their academic ability, family backgrounds, class, disability, gender or religion. Where each child enters school with a confidence that I belong and I am accepted for who I am.

Unfortunately, what children face in schools everyday is very different. They get a message very early on in school that there is a clear hierarchy on the basis of which the children are going to be treated. It is heartrending to see how some children gain prominence in schools and other children feel completely overlooked. There might be some children who get a message from very early on that 'you are not all right, something is wrong with you' and very gradually they start to understand that they do not really belong. They go to schools, slinking in the corridors, pushed to the corners in the classrooms and hiding behind their desks. These are the children who are hardly selected for any school events, whose creations do not go up on the noticeboard and whose names are not called out in the award ceremonies. These are the children whose names the teachers do not remember and who stay invisible for most of their school life. There are some who fight that invisibility by going to the other extreme of anger, aggression and pushing boundaries to be then thrown out of the system as being 'unsuitable'. Inclusion is just an empty word, a tick mark thrown around as it sounds so politically correct and suggests a progressive pedagogy.

As a teenager put it so eloquently, 'I feel I am like a ghost in school. Nobody looks at me, they look past me or they look through me. As if I am invisible.' As little children they really strive to become visible, trying desperately to get a rare smiley and 'well done' from the teacher. Middle school is the time they try even harder to fit in with their peers – trying to dress up like them, listen to the same music, talk like them, anxiously trying to make themselves photocopies of the more popular versions. By the time they reach senior school, they numb their pain by losing themselves in complete oblivion of invisibility, becoming withdrawn, depressed, drugged out, suicidal or anorexic (one of my clients with anorexia told me that she wanted to become invisible), whereas some resort to whatever they can do to make themselves more visible. They act out, become aggressive, resort to bullying tactics and take extreme risks. As if they are trying to shout and say, 'Look at me, I exist.'

Our schools are designed in an industrial model where children are part of an assembly line that starts at nursery and ends at Class XII. When there is stress, the speed of the conveyor belt is cranked up and the defective products are thrown out. We are all products of this industrial model and accept its way of working without any question. Educator Ken Robinson puts this metaphor brilliantly in his TED talk, 'Bring on the learning revolution'. A lot of schools like to boast about being 'inclusive' without even knowing what that concept means. We are failing our children in most schools. We are unable to provide emotionally safe zones to help them find their space and grow. School space matters a lot for children. Parents might go blue in the face telling the child she writes well but one word of recognition from her teacher can make her day. A smiley, a 'well done' in notebooks, clapping in the classroom after a show & tell, a story in the school magazine, applause in the assembly, a high five by his peers or a thump on the back by the teachers are the little spots of light every child seeks.

Have you seen the way the plants on the window sill turn towards the light, their stems and leaves pushing at the pane as if to soak in as much light as possible? The scientific term for that is heliotropism. C.G. Jung, iconic analytical psychotherapist, spoke of 'human heliotropism'. I believe that recognition and affirmation is the light that the children are seeking from the day they are born. They are pushing at the pane, 'look at me' but at times, we just turn away as we do not have the time or maybe we don't really care.

Nature

Human beings are biologically, emotionally, neurologically and spiritually wired to connect to nature. We have created artificial barriers from it but we are naturally part of it. Do you remember the last time you had a connect with nature? It could have been a jog in a lush green park early in the morning, a holiday in the mountains or a walk on a deserted beach? Can you recall the feeling of inner peace and a deep connection with your environment?

As a kid, most of my time was spent in the lap of nature with my friends. Whether it was looking for best orchards to steal plums from, or making makeshift tree houses, rolling down hills or taking a dip in the icy cold stream. Every winter, when my family visited Delhi for our annual holiday, I would get extremely intimidated by the city kids. They talked, walked and lived a different life and everything about them was so much more glossy and stylish. Now my kids are living that glossy life in the city and I feel so wistful that they cannot experience nature's roughness.

Richard Louv, in his book *Last Child in The Woods*, talks about a Nature Deficit Disorder that is slowly eating into our children's lives. There is more and more research on how taking children away from nature could be impacting their growth. In the last ten years, there has been a drastic slide from the real to the virtual. City kids need a healthy dose of nature to detoxify them from the churn of urban culture. They need a move from screen to green. In fact, we all need it big time.

We need to be creative to get green time back in their life. It could range from taking a birding holiday, encouraging wild-life photography, doing a short course in scuba diving, going for a family trek, or just spending a weekend spotting different kind of trees in the city. I remember a couple of years ago, my husband took both our kids for a course in herpetology to Croc banks and then to the rainforest in Agumbe research station. It was not an easy time for them (they had enough leech marks all over their body to vouch for that), but till date they talk about that as being their best holiday ever.

Children learn a lot about nature and saving the environment in their classrooms. However, it does not make sense till they are face to face with nature. It gives them a strong sense of connect, of belonging and, most importantly, they ask themselves this question, 'What am I doing to save it?' Recently, on my visit to a school, I was struck by the social and environmental awareness drives the school was carrying out. Aware of their after-school activities including theatre, art, dance, etc., I asked them about their most sought after club and was not surprised to hear the answer: 'Sustainability!'

I read somewhere that every child needs an adult who is crazy about him or her. I would go one step ahead and say that every child needs a village that is crazy about her. That watches out for her, takes interest in her, listens to her, celebrates her and makes her feel that she is worthy as she is and that she belongs.

I also believe that there are some children who are more vulnerable and we need to stretch ourselves a little more to provide them that village. These are children who have a disability, who have a learning difficulty or some other kind of neurodevelopmental handicap. These are children who have grown up thinking that they are lesser than others and adults in their lives struggle to understand their needs and cope with their pain or lack of understanding by blaming each other or worse, the children themselves. Children who have been adopted need a strong village too. Many a times, they carry in themselves a strong sense of rejection or abandonment at a cellular level. They need years of Connect and Community for them to let go of the rejection and believe in their own worthiness. This is also true for most children who have gone through abuse, pain or loss of any kind at an early age. They need adults who can put their pain or anxiety aside, or better still, heal themselves at the same time as healing the children by consistently giving the message, 'I hear you, I see you, I know you are in pain and I am there in your team to help you carry it for you'.

'There can be no keener revelation of society's soul than the way in which it treats its children.'

—Nelson Mandela

Reflection

1. What steps do you need to take to build a stronger 'emotionally safe zone' at home for your children?

2. How many caring adults does your child have in her 'village' who can provide the emotional vitamins for nourishment?

3. How would you want your children to describe the environment at home? What do you need to do every day to maintain that?

4. What conversation do you need to have with your child's school to ensure that he is being provided a nurturing space to grow and shine?

6

COMMITMENT

What is commitment? According to the thesaurus it means, 'The trait of sincere and steadfast fixity of purpose' or 'The act of binding yourself, intellectually and emotionally, to a course of action.' Yet, that still does not encapsulate it. It is so much more than that.

Commitment in parenting does not come from giving birth or adopting a child. It is a daily practice of immense grit. Commitment is to keep getting up after every one hour to feed the baby and not knowing for years what it is to have uninterrupted sleep at a stretch. Commitment is to spend back-breaking hours after work to play with your child when all you want to do is stretch on the sofa and sleep. Commitment is leaving the bawling child at the nursery and run so that he cannot see your tears. Commitment is to be there for your child even when the whole world is telling her that she is 'no good'. Commitment is to still smile and love your child with your whole heart after he has shouted that he hates you and can't wait to leave home. Commitment is to apologize to her and say, 'Sorry, I messed up as a parent, what can I do to make it better?'

Commitment in parenting requires immense compassion and courage. It takes compassion (for yourself and them) to trip, fall and then to get up again. Courage to pick up the pieces (theirs and yours) and say, 'It's all right, we will make it work.' Courage and compassion to celebrate your child and tell him you are worth it, when the whole world is saying otherwise.

Parenting is a soul journey that takes us places. Some of them are dark and frightening, some cold and lonely, some hot and angry, some shocking and prickly, but there will always be places that will be full of light and love. Those are the moments that carry us forward and expand us.

Each parent's journey is different and unique. For some it is a gentle trek, which goes uphill and becomes steep at times, but most of the time it is smooth. However, there are some for whom it is a bumpy terrain in rough weather right from the beginning. They trundle through the potholes, thick undergrowth and heavy vegetation, trying to make their own path in fading light.

My journey as a parent has been transformative to put it mildly. When our son, Nishat, was very little we realized that he was very different. His verbal skills were exceptional. At eighteen months, he could name all colours, recite nursery rhymes, speak in complex sentences, sing songs and rattle off names of various sea creatures at the drop of a hat. Our friends would, jokingly, ask us to put him in a circus (there was no Youtube then). When he was in preschool, his teachers were amazed at his ability to tell imaginative stories and his knack for out-of-the-box thinking. They loved him and he loved them. However, things changed when he joined formal school. Through the years, we could say that his teachers were always divided, either they loved him or they were completely bewildered by him. Words like 'exceptional poet', 'philosopher', 'deep thinker', 'lateral thinker', 'excellent orator', 'brilliant actor', 'walking encyclopedia' on one hand and 'dreamer', 'no sense of time', 'not reaching his potential' on the other, started dogging him. He was assessed and diagnosed with ADHD (Attention Deficit Hyperactivity Disorder) along with being Verbally Gifted. He was brilliant but he also had a disability. He was exceptional but he was not performing according to the society's norms. For most people, this paradox was difficult to fathom. Either you are this or that, you can't be both. But he was, he is and he will continue to be. Like many other sparkling minds out there!

Nishat has taught my husband Amit and me more about children than anything else in the world: their amazing minds and parenting these minds. I remember when he was about eight, I was playing this game with him where I kept asking him questions like, 'Who is your best friend?'

'Who is your favourite aunt/uncle?'

'Who is your favourite teacher?'

'Which teacher do you not like?'

After listening to me for some time, he said, 'Mum, why do you want to see the world in black and white, good and bad? I see people as rainbows with different colours!' That's what we do, we pigeonhole children in different boxes as good and bad, bright and dull, high IQ and low IQ, smart and dumb. How different would it be if, like a prism, we learned to catch the light in each child and see the rainbow that she or he carries? Going back to Nishat, his journey has been unique. He has had more than his share of bumps, falls and struggles but that has not stopped him from moving ahead. He has gone through his dark phases but that has not dimmed his light.

The reason I have shared my journey is that there are many other parents out there who go through one day at a time with a heavy heart and feet. Their stories could be slightly different from mine, but the pain in their heart as they look at their child who will just 'not fit in' is immense. I want to tell those parents that your child does not need to fit in, he or she is worthy as she or he is. It is said that we need to look at the glass as half full and not half empty, I would go one step further and say that forget the half full and half empty and just look at the sparkling water!

All Joy But No Fun

I really enjoyed reading a book on parenthood (not parenting) by Jennifer Senior called *All Joy and No Fun, The Paradox of Modern Day Parenthood*! Jennifer Senior highlights how parenting can end up depriving the parents of the experience of 'flow' (essential component for happiness as I explained in Care). Flow is the state of magical engagement where the person experiences being in the zone as their mastery and skill in the task matches the challenge posed. A musician might experience it while practising a new composition, a writer, lost deep in his book, might feel it while writing and a teacher, while passionately explaining a new concept to the class. An important part of flow is that the person loses the sense of time and experiences complete immersion in that moment. Parents struggle to experience flow as parenting can end up being repetitive, lonely and monotonous.

As a parent of a two year old once told me in despair, 'Every morning the day looms large in front of me. Same old routine, same old whining, fights and demands. I don't do much through the day but I am exhausted.' I remember when my kids were little, for me, going to work was like taking a break. At work I was in a territory that challenged me to master skills, use my brain and be in the flow. However, no matter how much I loved my kids, flow was a rare commodity at home. If you have sat with a toddler for one hour at a stretch just passing the ball, or constructing and breaking towers or 'cooked' the nth meal with the kitchen set then you know what I mean.

That is what commitment is. Getting out of bed every morning and deciding to be the best parent you can be that day. If you have a child who is wired differently due to a learning difficulty, autism or any other neurodevelopmental delay or physical disability then your journey becomes even more tumultuous. The lows can be often and completely drain you out but when the highs happen, and when they do happen, they can be the most uplifting and joyous experiences. As a parent of a child with autism once told me, 'I have learned to experience such deep sorrow. But these sorrows have also deepened my ability to experience joys of the kind I had never experienced before in my life.' That's why a hike in the rough terrain with its bumps and potholes is exhausting but more exhilarating than a walk in a manicured park.

To the parents of children who are wired differently, I would always urge that you need to crank up all the five Cs to a higher level. You need to dig deep to connect, coach one step at a time, care for yourself, build a caring community and commit at a higher level. Stop apologizing for your children and start advocating for them. Have faith in them, deep faith in the light in each one of them. If you are the only one who sees that light then let it be so but do not let anybody else dim that light for you.

This is for all parents who have a child with a disability:

Are you ready? To live your life, one day at a time? At times from one hour to another, moment to moment? To accept that future is a chasm that will maybe (definitely) be an adventure like no other? To see the sparkle in your child when others just see shadows? To open your arms wide and your heart even wider, when others shrink away? To smile and blow away the worries of the others? To let your smile become your tears and the tears become your smile? To repeat, repeat and repeat again? And then maybe once again? To take another angle, outlook, perspective, world-view that you had never seen before? To keep taking leaps of faith with your eyes shut? And lastly, most importantly, knowing deep in your heart that you would not have it any other way?

Andrew Solomon, one of my favourite writers, talks about 'forging meaning' in one of his awe-inspiring TED talks, 'How the worst moments in our lives make us who we are'. He talks about how crucial it is for us to take our pain, our adversity, our deepest fears and forge some meaning out of it. Your child with a disability might have made you experience pain but at the same time empowered you to become a passionate advocate for inclusive education. Your own abuse at an early age might help you forge meaning and move you to commit to work towards safer childhoods.

Another of my favourite authors, Haruki Murakami, puts it as, 'Pain is inevitable, suffering is optional.' So, don't wish your pain away. As Andrew Solomon so eloquently explains it, 'But if you banish the dragons, you banish the heroes.'

'Parenting is a mirror in which we get to see the best of ourselves, and the worst; the richest moments of living, and the most frightening.'
—Jon Kabat-Zinn, scientist, writer and meditation teacher

Before I end, I would again like to highlight some of my deep beliefs about parenting.

Each child is wired and inspired differently – Your child is unique, original and there is no one like him in this world. Try to understand his wiring. What makes him tick? What is he passionate about? What are his strengths? What are his affinities and what are his assets? What does he struggle with? What are his frailties? What helps him to learn? Move away from cookie-cutter, black and white and look at the rainbow in your child.

Inside-out approach – Whenever you are going through a difficult phase in parenting, shift the focus from the child to yourself. What am I feeling right now? Am I being driven by deep-rooted anxiety that is coming in the way of connecting to my child? Is it more about my feelings of inadequacy than about her difficulties? Am I being driven by what the society expects me to do rather than what I really believe in? Is it more about my needs or hers? Am I being the best parent I can be?

Kids will do well if they can – Children are like sunflowers, turning their heads towards the light, nudging away slight hurdles as they rise high and find their place under the sun. Every child wants his or her place under the sun and if he or she does not find it then we have to find out what is holding him or her back. Is it the some hidden miswiring, is it the school, is it the emotional environment at home? There is nothing like 'he does not want to do well', 'she just wants to be difficult'. What is stopping your sunflower from growing? Look in the undergrowth, look at the soil, check the nutrition provided, pull out the weeds, make space and then step back. You have done your job and now just keep faith that the growth will happen at its own pace.

What you focus on grows – This is a big one! How do you practice your art of selective watering? Are you doing enough of it for yourself? Are you mindfully watering the wholesome seeds in your key relationships? Are you giving enough messages of 'you are worthy as you are' to your child? Are you marvelling enough at the sparkling light that they carry with them rather than getting lost in the shadows where the light does not reach?

There are times when I feel such a deep sense of awe looking at my children. One way taller than me and the other not too far behind. I can't get over the fact that I gave birth to them and that they are the same babies I could fit into the crook of my arm. It amazes me that they are human beings with their own thinking, beliefs and way of living. They have strong views on music, movies, food, clothes, politics, religion, environment, poverty, education and yes, of course, parenting. They question, they wonder, they challenge and they decide.

Commitment is also about finding ourselves in our children and accepting how different they are from us. When I think of my relationship with my mother, I struggle to put a finger on what has bound us together for all these years. I left my small town in the mountains at the age of fifteen and have never gone back to live there again. Yet, there is still a home for me there, where my mother lives. Paradoxically we are so different from each other but so alike. As a child and, later, as a teenager, I could talk to her very openly as I knew she would understand. As if she had travelled the same path and that was enough for us to connect.

As Thich Nhat Hanh, the Zen Buddhist master puts it, 'It is true that you are your mother, you are the continuation of your mother and that is the way of inviting you to look deeply into yourself.'

Looking deeply into oneself can be tough when the connection is so deep. As a child, every fear, tear or angry look from my mother had the power to send me into a flap. Adolescence was a stage when I very typically and deliberately started doing everything I could to show how different I was to her. When I had my children, especially my daughter, my relationship with my mother took on another rich dimension. I am sure many of you would echo the sentiment that it is only when you become a mother that you appreciate what your mother is all about!

And as I have grown older and built my own identities, and have become mindful of my own emotional reactions, I am aware of my mother's voice that I still carry with me. My mother being the person she is, has made this voice a mellow yet empowering presence. She is me and I am her.

Having a son first was so beautiful, but there was always that little bit of doubt as being a woman I did not know what it was like to be a boy. I had grown up with an older brother but despite that I was a little clueless. That was a journey I was not familiar with at all. But when I see my daughter now, I am filled with immense wonder. I can see my own reflection in her. When she is shy and all tongue-tied in social situations, when oblivious to our calling out her name we find her snuggled up with a fat book in a corner, when she picks up a silly word and keeps repeating it gleefully, giggling so much that she chokes and falls off the sofa. She is me and I am her.

Yet I am eagerly waiting for the day when she will tell me, 'I am so different from you', the same way I told my mother. And that is fine with me as it defines the circle of life.

As Rabindranath Tagore put it so beautifully in one of his poems, 'I keep losing you with a hope to find you again in a new way.' With trepidation, I am waiting to lose my daughter to discover her again.

I do not categorize myself as a good or bad parent. I believe parenting is a daily practice, a mindful practice that I work on every day. There are many days when I go to sleep with a contented heart, as I believe that I have been the best parent I could be and there are days when I end the day with a heavy heart. However, I have learned to be self-compassionate, stay light on my toes and just take one day at a time.

Parental GPS

These are some questions, which help me to stay on track, especially when I am going through a rough patch.

1. What does my emotional bank account with my child look like?
2. Am I energizing her wholesome seeds?
3. Am I accepting his worthiness as he is, or am I wishing he needs to change for himself to win that from me?
4. Am I connecting to her strengths, assets and affinities?
5. Am I connecting from my heart and soul?
6. Am I convinced myself?
7. Am I letting negativity seep in?
8. Are my expectations unrealistic?
9. Am I taking one step at a time?
10. Am I getting too much into telling and not letting her reflect, make choices and be responsible?
11. Am I taking care of myself?

12. Am I building a nurturing community for my child?
13. Am I willing to make a paradigm shift and make parenting about working on myself rather than my child?
14. How committed am I?

Parenting is like organic gardening to me. Each sapling in the garden is different and unique. As gardeners we have to make sure we understand the needs of each and every plant. Some have deeper roots so they need more water, some need shade, some need regular pruning and some need more space. Our job is to focus on what we need to do to provide them the best environment for growth. Weeds, pests and bad weather are inevitable and a given. A passionate gardener will tell you that the best job of being a gardener is to do your job and then step back and enjoy the beauty of the plants as they grow. Each one at its own pace and in its inimitable way!

Parenting is a soul craft, a journey which moves both inward and outward. The lows are unbearable and the highs are unimaginable. So let us commit to moving forward mindfully yet playfully. Remember, it's not about the kids, it's about us!

RECOMMENDED READING

Bagley, Sharon. *Train Your Mind, Change Your Brain: How a New Science Reveals Our Extraordinary Potential to Transform Ourselves*. Ballantine Books, 2007.

Brown, Brené. *Gifts of Imperfection*. Penguin, 2013.

Brown, Brené. *Daring Greatly*. Penguin, 2013.

Brown, Stuart. *Play: How It Shapes the Brain, Opens the Imagination, and Invigorates the Soul*. Penguin, 2009.

Coyle, Daniel. *The Talent Code: Greatness isn't born. It's grown*. Arrow, 2010.

Csikszentmihalyi, Mihaly. *Flow: The Psychology of Optimal Experience*. Harper Perennial Modern Classics, 2008.

Dweck, Carol. *Mindset: The New Psychology of Success*. Ballantine Books, 2007.

Glasser, Howard. *Notching up the Nurtured Heart Approach*. Nurtured Heart Publications, 2011.

Goleman, Daniel. *Emotional Intelligence: Why it Can Matter More Than IQ*. Bloomsbury, 1996.

Greene, Ross. *The Explosive Child: A New Approach for*

Understanding and Parenting Easily Frustrated, Chronically Inflexible Children (Fifth Edition). Harper, 2014.

Hanh, Thich Nhat. *The Miracle of Mindfulness: The Classic Guide to Meditation by the World's Most Revered Master*. Random House, 2008.

Hanh, Thich Nhat. *Transformation and Healing: Sutra on the Four Establishments of Mindfulness*. Parallel Press, 2006.

Kahneman, Daniel. *Thinking, Fast and Slow*. Farrar, Straus and Giroux, 2013.

Marshall, Mervin. *Parenting Without Stress: How to Raise Responsible Kids While Keeping a Life of Your Own*. Piper Press, 2010.

Ricard, Matthieu. *Happiness: A Guide to Developing Life's Most Important Skill*. Little, Brown and Company, 2007.

Roth, Tom. *Eat Move Sleep: How Small Choices Lead to Big Changes*. Missionday, 2013.

Senior, Jennifer. *All Joy and No Fun: The Paradox of Modern Parenthood*. Ecco, 2015.

Solomon, Andrew. *Far from tree*. Simon & Schuster, 2012.

Tolle, Eckhart. *The Power of Now: A Guide to Spiritual Enlightenment*. Namaste Publishing, 2004.

Tolle, Eckhart. *A New Earth: Awakening to Your Life's Purpose*. Penguin, 2008.

ACKNOWLEDGEMENTS

I do not think a book like this can be the contribution of just a single individual. I am forever grateful to the amazing children and their parents I have met and worked with over the years. The rainbow of stories they brought with them made me a witness to amazing grit, courage, resilience, suffering, kindness and, above all, sheer indomitable love.

To the HarperCollins editorial team – publisher Karthika, Debasri and Bidisha – for connecting to my ideas so easily and graciously. To cover designer, Bonita, for her creative ideas and patience to deal with my tendency to get fastidious.

Heartfelt thanks to Sanghamitra Chakraborty and her brilliant team at Prevention for helping me hone my writing skills. Manjira Dutta and the Good Housekeeping team for the creative range they come up with every month.

A big thank you to my mother, who I can give the title, 'Best Mother in the World' without any hesitation. I continue to marvel at her joie de vivre every day. To my father, who weathered my angst and intensity for many years with grace.

To my brother Shailesh for that super sibling bond and childhood spent discussing books, music and life. Namrata for being a sister I never had. Rana for being Rana and for always being there. Mimi and Manas for having the courage to parent differently. I truly admire both of you. Monica for her quiet and strong presence in our family.

To Bappa, who has redefined what a father can be and Ma, who defined what love for children is all about.

To Rukmini, our wonderful Mishi, who has the uncanny knack of connecting to the spark in every child.

To Titli, Tan, Tia, Joey and Sushrut, you are the sparks in my life and inspiration for 'each child is wired and inspired differently'.

To my Children First family whose zest, commitment and creativity keeps me going. Kavita for giving me strength and from whom I have learned so much and whose PJs are legendary. Ankita whose brilliance, warmth and wackiness rejuvenates me so much and Prachi for being an emotionally safe sounding board for so many of my bizarre ideas. Lavina, Jonaki and Soumini for being our gorgeous pillars and Ritu, Iti, Tara, Noor, Kim and rest of the team for making CF what it is.

To Thich Nhat Hanh, Buddhist monk, poet, author, teacher and peace activist whose mindfulness practice helped me water the wholesome seeds in others and myself.

To Catherine Brown for introducing me to the Nurtured Heart Approach and to Howard Glasser for making my practice deeper.

To the Beatles for their dazzling idea, 'All You Need Is Love', which I have carried with me forever.

To all the awesome teachers I have met in my journey. As a parent I salute you – Manika Ma'am and her dynamic team – Janani, Piku, Roopa, Rati, Neeta and so many more. Thanks for being the inspiration for my next book on power of teachers!

To Geet for being a crazy, funny, loving friend and a super single mum.

To my amazing tribe of friends, family and colleagues across the globe who are the lifeblood of the community I so believe in.

Deep gratitude to my amazing children, Nishat and Anya, who gently and patiently helped me grow up and learn to live wholeheartedly.

To Amit, this book is as much his as mine as every thought expressed here has been discussed, pondered over, mused on and woven together with him. Taking some lines from another of our favourite bands, Queen: *'Ooh, you make me live. You, you're my best friend!'*